Delightful! Inspiring! Practical! Challenging! Through real-life experiences and awe-inspiring quotes from spiritual masters, Kathy Hendricks helps us to explore how balance enables us to respond to our off-kilter moments in peace, convergence, and blessing. Spiritual balance—the reality of living in healthy, whole-ly, and holy ways—is illustrated throughout the book with a consideration of the rich tradition of our spiritual practices as well as innovative, creative ones. As we journey through the grace-filled circus of life, we will be drawn to read this book again and again—for encouragement and nourishment, for comfort and challenge.

JANET SCHAEFFLER, OP,
author, adult faith formation and retreat facilitator

Woven around the metaphor of a circus and lessons culled from the author's yearlong trip visiting forty-eight states, *Seeking Spiritual Balance* is definitely entertaining. But more important, it is a valuable self-help book, especially for anyone longing for stability in the midst of a hectic life. Kathy Hendricks's solid, practical advice for living well, along with numerous quotations from wise spiritual writers, make this book one to dip into and savor time and again. An appendix of various prayer methods is an added benefit.

MARY KATHLEEN GLAVICH, SND, *author of*
The Catholic Way to Pray** and **Praying on Empty

This is an essential read for anyone navigating a demanding life. Kathy Hendricks shares the wisdom she gleaned about spiritual balance from a yearlong sabbatical. With intriguing stories, engaging metaphors, and potential practices, *Seeking Spiritual Balance in an Off-Kilter World* is an excellent dialogue partner for anyone wishing to establish or fine-tune their spiritual equilibrium.

BARBARA ANNE RADTKE, *Instructional Designer, Boston College School of Theology and Ministry*

※

This book is full of practical know-how in living the Christian life. It talks about how to use Sabbath rest, acquire self-knowledge and mindfulness, stay aware of the presence of God in us and around us, and keep our balance while dealing with multitasking, sensory overload, excess baggage, fears, and threats to our peace of mind. It teaches us to join the great circus of life in all of its glorious diversity and to draw others into its circle of forgiveness, compassion, and mercy.

FR. DAVID KNIGHT, *author of* **A Fresh Look at Confession: Why it Really is Good for the Soul**

SEEKING SPIRITUAL BALANCE

IN AN OFF-KILTER WORLD

Seeking Spiritual Balance

in an Off-Kilter World

HOW TO FIND YOUR "CENTER" IN THE CIRCUS OF LIFE

Kathy Hendricks

TWENTY-THIRD PUBLICATIONS

twentythirdpublications.com

All Bible passages from the New American Bible unless otherwise noted.

"Grant Me an Enchantment of Heart" by Ted Loder, is from Ted Loder,
Guerrillas of Grace: Prayers for the Battle (Minneapolis: Augsburg Books, 1981).
Used with permission. All rights reserved.

The Poem "CAMAS LILIES," copyright by Lynn Ungar.
Used with permission. All rights reserved.

Cover Illustration: Superstock.com / Tim Teebken / Exactostock-1598

TWENTY-THIRD PUBLICATIONS
1 Montauk Avenue, Suite 200, New London, CT 06320
(860) 437-3012 » (800) 321-0411 » www.twentythirdpublications.com

ISBN: 978-1-62785-256-2
Library of Congress Catalog Card Number: 2017932940
Printed in the U.S.A.

 A division of Bayard, Inc.

Dedication

FOR RON

Thanks for the journey
of a lifetime.

Contents

"*Sometimes I think God wants there to be a circus so he can show there's another way to respond.*"

TONY DUNGY
FOOTBALL COACH
AND AUTHOR

"Ladies and gentlemen, boys and girls. Welcome to the greatest show on earth."

Thus goes the typical ringmaster's invitation to eager audiences waiting for the circus to begin. It's one thing to sit in the grandstand waiting to be entertained. It's quite another to find ourselves in center ring, desperately trying to keep pace with the performances others expect of us. When life feels like a three-ring circus, we find ourselves teetering on a tightrope strung between chaotic activity and daily regimens. We are thrown off-kilter by too many responsibilities to juggle and people to keep happy. Where can we go to restore a sense of equilibrium? How do we find and maintain spiritual balance in the midst of busy, active lives?

These are the questions I want to address in the course of this book. Using the circus as a metaphor, I describe strategies for creating a bit of balance while also rediscovering the circus performer of our dreams. As you make your way through each chapter you will find questions that invite you to reflect on your own off-kilter moments and ways to pull them into balance. The last part of the book offers an Appendix with a description of practices that can further the quest for spiritual balance.

The first part of the book invites you to step out of center ring and move toward the periphery where the soul can find rest and rejuvenation. By the book's end, I hope you will find yourself ready to reenter center ring with a spirit that is rested and rejuvenated, and with a fresh sense of playfulness and adventure.

Step right up and let us begin.

CHAPTER ONE

Exiting Center Ring

WHAT THROWS YOU OFF BALANCE? Any number of answers might come to mind. Perhaps it's time—or the lack of it—and the feeling of continually running behind schedule. It might be responsibilities at home or work, in church, the neighborhood, or civic community. Then there is the upheaval accompanying the unexpected—a sudden illness or disability, the death of a loved one or loss of a job, an unanticipated move, change of boss, dip in income, or breakdown of a major appliance. Even the positive changes in life can have an unsettling effect, requiring us to switch gears, adjust to new rhythms and routines, and regain our footing.

Beyond our personal experiences lies a world set off-kilter by unstable markets, perpetual wars, and political polarization. Technology multiplies our exposure to local, national, and global news while, at the same time, requiring new devices to access it. All of these, in turn, take time to learn and then to manage so that we are not thrown further off balance by the evaporation of even more time and energy.

It's like living in a three-ring circus. What better metaphor for the off-kilter life than a circus? Simultaneous performances vie for the audience's attention, which, in turn, bounces back and forth from center ring to the rafters and then to the sidelines. It's not much different from the demands that come from overactive toddlers, domineering bosses, critical in-laws, frazzled spouses, annoying coworkers, noisy neighbors, and surly adolescents. Each one might merit attention or insist upon it. Either way, the attempt to keep everything functioning is exhausting and overwhelming. Embedded within the circus metaphor are the performers, each having a specific role to play:

- The juggler, keeping multiple items aloft without dropping them.

- The tightrope walker, treading a fine line in order to not to topple off the high wire.

- The lion tamer, risking life and limb while facing down wild beasts.

- The trapeze artist, swinging from one thing to the next, often without a safety net.

- The strong (wo)man, shouldering enormous amounts of weight.

- The clown, assuring everyone else's happiness through relentless good humor.

- The ringmaster, keeping the acts in sync and the onlookers informed and engaged.

Assuming any one of these roles is a feat. What happens when multiple performances are expected from us? How do we keep our act together?

Few of us have the luxury of choosing the circus performer we want to be. Instead, we take on different roles in order to fulfill the multiple demands and responsibilities that come with a family, job, religious affiliation, and community involvement. We can end up operating in all three circus rings at the same time, taking on, in each case, a different role to suit the expectations of the onlookers as well as ourselves:

Ring 1—At Home
Consider the performers we become within the circle of family, friends, and other intimate and professional relationships. Who do those closest to us expect us to be? For some it is the strong man or woman who holds up the rest of the clan even when the weight becomes insupportable. For others, it is the juggler, managing the busy schedules of the household without letting anything drop. Some of us are expected to play the clown by keeping family, friends, coworkers, and colleagues happy and in touch with each other. Whatever the performance, the expectations of others put us in an off-balance position as outside demands outweigh our capacity to meet them.

Ring 2—In the World
The expectations we place on ourselves can be even more intense than those imposed upon us by others. Those with a strong need for control step into the role of ringmaster in the mistaken belief that they can keep the lives of family members and social circles in order. Others put on the bravado of the lion tamer, reluctant to allow anyone else to see the beasts that threaten their equilibrium

and thus expose their need for assistance. Still others swing wildly from one task to the next, eager to demonstrate how competent they are at multitasking. Without a safety net of support and the ability to establish boundaries, these people are at risk of losing their grip and suffering catastrophic physical, emotional, psychological, and spiritual injury.

Ring 3—On Our Own

The ring we may enter the least is also the most necessary for spiritual balance; it entails becoming the performer of our dreams. Each circus act that flows from natural talent and intention takes on an air of grace and beauty. Consider the concentration and inner anchoring that allows a tightrope walker to not only cross a high wire, but also to dance on it. There is the flexibility of the trapeze artist, the dexterity of the juggler, and the self-confidence of the ringmaster; the courage of the lion tamer, endurance of the strong woman, and lightheartedness of the clown. When we concentrate on and work with our strengths, we find ourselves capable of incredible feats. We also rediscover our playful nature.

Life can go off-kilter when we operate out of all three circus rings at the same time. If the expectations we have of ourselves and the ones others have of us are disparate, we are bound to run headlong into disappointment and frustration. Add to the mix the performer we long to be, and how lonely, isolated, and wistful we feel when that kind of life is forever beyond our reach.

What does it take, then, to get our act together so that we temper the expectations of others and those we place on ourselves? How do we stay realistic about our limitations while still holding onto our dreams and tapping into our best selves?

STEPPING OUT

We cannot expect life to fall into balance overnight. We can, however, take a step in that direction.

The circus is an itinerant life. It moves from place to place, pitching a tent for a temporary series of engagements before moving on. Traveling circuses often take place outside of the town limits, making them peripheral to the main center of activity. In order to attend, people move toward the outskirts and gather under the Big Top. The circus draws both performers and audience away from life as usual.

"Running away to join the circus" was once a popular idiom for those wishing to escape the humdrum and tedious routine of life. It embraced that itinerant life as an antidote to boredom and the mundane. It stepped away from life as usual.

My husband, Ron, and I didn't join the circus, but we did take an intentional step out of center ring. In 2008 we embarked on the journey of a lifetime. It came about as a result of lengthy planning and dreaming. We sold our house and traded our two cars for a small SUV. After whittling down our possessions, we placed most of them in storage and loaded the rest in the car. Then we embarked on a major road trip. We had few particular plans except to get to all forty-eight of the contiguous United States and to as many national parks as we could. Our travels took close to a year and added 40,000 miles to the odometer.

Besides providing an opportunity to see many beautiful places, the trip afforded a radical change of pace. For an entire year I didn't run a vacuum cleaner or attend a meeting. Ron indulged his passion for photography and amassed a collection of over 20,000 digital pictures. I composed hundreds of logs, blogs, and journal letters, none of which were subject to deadlines. As a couple, we gave in to the restlessness that has kept us together for the past forty years. Traveling together is what we do best.

2008 was an off-kilter year for the country, making the timing of our travels significant in unforeseen ways. Besides the U.S. being enmeshed in two wars, the national economy was receding, and a vitriolic presidential campaign was heating up. While banks failed, markets crashed, and the red-blue divide between the states inten-sified, Ron and I rode along in relative oblivion, tuning in and out of the news when we felt like it. Our travels gave us time off the grid in which to ramble along backroads and to watch each day unfold. It was a time of adventure, discovery, and simple living.

SABBATH TIME

Before our departure, I discussed the trip with our pastor. "How wonderful," he said. "You are going on sabbatical." The term took me by surprise. I long associated sabbaticals with those in academia or with clergy who took an extended leave to study and reflect. It never seemed like something within my reach. As we moved into the rhythm of the road, however, it began to make sense, particu-larly when linked to the concept of Sabbath.

In his book *Sabbath*, Wayne Mueller notes that "keeping the Sabbath holy" is the only one of the Ten Commandments starting with the word "remember." Sabbath, he writes, is "a way of being in time where we remember who we are, remember what we know and taste the gifts of spirit and eternity." Thus, to keep the Sabbath is to step away from the regular routine and lay aside work and worry in order to find a place of rest and rejuvenation. In doing so, we find and remember our true center once again. Making it an ongoing practice increases our ability to strike a balance between work and rest, be-tween routines and recreation, between immersion in an active, busy life and withdrawal to its passive edges. Like the trapeze artist, swing-ing through the air with "the greatest of ease," we find that Sabbath keeping doesn't make one part of our lives worthwhile and the rest of it a waste. Instead it affirms the importance of being both participants and onlookers, of valuing the multiplicity of our responsibilities and of setting boundaries around them. As we grow more adept at striking a balance between activity and passivity, it becomes habitual to exit center ring on a regular basis.

Jesus was a model Sabbath keeper. He withdrew on a regular

basis for refreshment and renewal through prayer and time with family and friends. He knew when it was time to exit the center ring of movement and activity. "He didn't ask permission, nor did he leave anyone behind 'on call,' or even let his disciples know where he was going. Jesus obeyed a deeper rhythm. When the moment for rest had come, the time for healing was over. He would simply stop, retire to a quiet place, and pray" (Mueller).

All of this makes sense on an intuitive level. What, then, makes Sabbath so difficult to remember? For one thing, keeping the Sabbath appears to be an outdated and unrealistic practice in a society operating like a three-ring circus. Even for those who maintain a religious practice, it is easy to fudge on the concept by making a perfunctory stop at a church or synagogue and then proceeding with a weekend full of frenetic activity. Sabbath keeping as a *suggestion* rather than a *commandment* becomes the norm. Some may also find the concept of a full day devoted to rest daunting. Author Barbara Brown Taylor recalls the Sabbath restrictions placed on her while growing up in the South. She was not allowed to ride her bike, wear jeans, or go to the movies. The commandment then meant: "Remember the Sabbath and keep it boring" (*An Altar in the World*).

*How do you make Sabbath keeping
a part of your life?*

THE LIBERATION OF SABBATH

The original concept of Sabbath is rooted in a journey. In the Book of Exodus Moses is given the Ten Commandments during the forty-year trek that took the Israelites out of slavery in Egypt to the Promised Land. This linked the meaning of Sabbath to that of liberation. The longer the road, however, the more prone the Israelites were to forgetting what their enslaved lives entailed. In order to remember, they had to step out anew each day. "Sabbath is the true God's gift to those who wish to rest and be free—and who are willing to guard those same gifts for every living thing in their vicinity as well" (Barbara Brown Taylor). Thus, a recognition of Sabbath's importance is not just for our own individual recreation; it has profound meaning for a world gone seriously off-kilter.

It takes intention to find spiritual balance. We must be willing to take the first step and then another... and another. No one wants to be enslaved by the clock, by overload, stress, or the crushing aftermath of pain, loss, and heartache. Nevertheless, it is only human to hold back, opting for the seen over the unseen, the known over the unknown. It's like venturing onto a high wire where the fear of falling is matched only by the trepidation of learning what may lie on the other side. The only way forward is one careful step at a time. This is what the ancient Israelites did. It's also what every traveler and circus performer must do, mile after mile, performance after performance. The only way to proceed is with trust that the day's needs will be met. Over time, the road widens, opening up to more practical ways of maintaining balance.

Sabbath time not only liberates us from unrelenting activity but also from the demon of anxiety that often accompanies it. On the first night of our yearlong trip, I spent a wakeful night at our hotel in Santa Fe, New Mexico, staring at the cracks in the ceiling and second-guessing our decision. I ticked off a mental list of all that could go wrong—carjacking, accidents, injuries, death... Without a home to go back to, my anxieties reached fever pitch. What were we thinking? The next morning I poured out my fears to Ron. He listened and then reminded me that the only way to make such an ambitious trip was one day at a time. His words proved to be true. They also apply to any venture out of center ring. Moving forward in trust is the best way to embark on any journey, be it physical or spiritual.

My litany of "what ifs" characterizes the kind of preoccupation that sets us off-kilter. Before we even depart, we fill the journey with concerns about the crises that could befall us and how they will lead to failure and potential danger. Consider the juggler overly worried about dropping the balls or the tightrope walker afraid to step out onto the high wire. If Ron and I had given in to my anxieties, we would have missed the trip of a lifetime. In his book *Making All Things New*, Henri Nouwen connects the scourge of anxiety to an imbalanced spiritual life. "One way to express the spiritual crisis of our time is to say that most of us have an address but cannot be found there. We know where we belong, but we keep being pulled away in many directions, as if we were homeless." Worrying not only fragments our lives but also keeps us from finding our true center.

One of the great paradoxes in the Bible is how often people were called away from their homes—their places of security and stability—in order to walk the high wire of faith. The Exodus journey is one example. The call to Abraham and Sarah is another. At a time in their lives when they might have kicked back and enjoyed the time that remained in their lives, God called them to travel to an unknown land. "Go forth," he told them and then provided no map or description of their final destination. They obeyed with a bit of trepidation but also with a trust that outweighed their anxiety.

Ron and I weren't, like Abraham and Sarah, in our mid-70s when we set off on our cross-country trip; we also weren't exactly footloose and fancy-free. I continued to work as a contributing writer for William H. Sadlier, a job made all the easier by online communication and mobile phones. This made our travels financially feasible but meant I still had to meet deadlines on work projects and participate electronically in editorial meetings. It wasn't this activity—a part of my own center ring—that threatened to throw the whole venture off-balance, however. It was my first-night jitters about what might go wrong. Once I let go of my anxiety and we both admitted the futility of mapping out the entire expedition, we reveled in the freedom of the road. What a great way to view the entire journey of life.

A JOURNEY OF THE HEART

Taking the first step on any journey requires *courage*. The word itself comes from a root meaning "heart." Looking back, I see how stepping out on our trip was also pursuing our "heart's desire." Perhaps this same longing stirred Abraham and Sarah, Moses and the enslaved Israelites, and the disciples who jumped out of their boat in order to follow Jesus. The decision to exit center ring and move toward a more balanced spiritual life comes first and foremost from the heart.

Let me be clear. The corrective to an off-kilter life doesn't necessarily entail an ambitious road trip or joining the circus, tempting as those options might be. In the years since Ron and I settled back in Colorado after our lengthy sojourn, I have reflected on some of the lessons learned from stepping out of center ring. One is the value of "peripheral living." This is an intentional practice in which we detach from frenetic pursuits, from noise and negativity, from toxic relationships, and from commitments we no long need or care about. It also draws us toward the liberation of simplicity. Once we reach the periphery through regular periods of Sabbath rest and reflection, we begin to recognize the center rings we no longer need or want to enter again.

The manner in which we step out of center ring also matters. In making a conscious choice to sell our house and leave most of our possessions behind, Ron and I chose to free ourselves from the worries of ownership. This is another aspect of peripheral living. Dragging along our "stuff"—be it physical, mental, or emotional—is hardly the way to exit center ring. As the comedian George Carlin put it, "Just 'cause you got the monkey off your back doesn't mean the circus has left town." There has to be an intentional effort to leave behind the baggage that weighs us down or keeps us anchored to anxiety and fear. Offloading it gives way to a wider mindset, one that makes the first step exhilarating.

Moving to the periphery isn't a complete withdrawal from life's activities but one in which we become mindful of the moment. It requires walking a tightrope between two time-honored spiritual states of the heart—contemplation* and action. Holding the two together requires a delicate balance, something we learn from circus performers who do so with grace and ease.

FOR REFLECTION AND DISCUSSION

*Which circus performer do I most resemble—
at home, in the world, and in my dreams?*

*What center ring do I need to exit on occasion in order
to reclaim a sense of spiritual balance?*

What is preventing me from taking the first step?

*Spiritual practices designated by an asterisk are explored more fully in the Appendix, "From Performance to Practice."

CHAPTER TWO

Balancing Acts

The Gospel of Luke includes a wonderful story about walking the tightrope between action and contemplation (Luke 10:38–42). The tension of the tightly strung high wire is embodied in two sisters—Martha and Mary. One is busy preparing a meal, and the other is seated at the feet of Jesus. Martha violates a critical rule of hospitality when she asks her guest to intercede in a family dispute. "Lord, do you not care that my sister has left me by myself to do the serving? Tell her to help me." When Jesus chides Martha over her agitation around Mary's behavior, he doesn't tell her to stop what she is doing. Instead he challenges her to see *how* she is doing it. Martha takes on the role of the strong woman—bearing the heft of household responsibilities. While it is a necessary task, her resentment toward Mary only adds to the weight she carries.

I once saw a dramatic depiction of this account in which Mary extends her hand to Martha and gently guides her to a place on the floor. It was a striking way to portray the gentle invitation to enjoy the "better part" that Jesus names. In his book *Gratefulness, the Heart of Prayer,* David Steindl-Rast writes how our activities create something akin to a centrifugal force. "They tend to pull us from our center into peripheral concerns. And the faster the spin of our daily round of activities, the stronger the pull. We need to anchor ourselves in the silent center of our heart." The trap of the overactive life—one illustrated by Martha's beleaguered plea for help—is one of the most common reasons for feeling off-kilter. The movement from center ring to the periphery is an intentional one in which we don't give ourselves over to tangential concerns but to a centeredness in God.

The late John Mogabgab, editor of *Weavings* magazine, once described Jesus as a "denizen of the edges." It's a striking description of the way in which Jesus walked the tightrope between engagement and withdrawal, community and solitude,* talking and listening, work and play. "Jesus can live on the edge because he lives from a center radiant with God's love for him and for all creation. There his treasure lies, there his heart abides, from there the boundaries of his heart expand to transform every edge into a potential center of God's untamed grace. As the Spirit of God gradually conforms our hearts to the heart of Jesus, we begin to move away from the centers of world and self to edges where God is doing a new thing" ("Editor's Introduction," *Weavings,* XIII, No. 4). No wonder Mary was so attracted to Jesus and chose to simply sit at his feet, taking in his presence as well as his teachings. The "helping hand" Martha actually needed was the one I saw enacted in the dramatization of this lovely story. It was one of invitation to move toward the edges where something new and wondrous could be worked in her life.

At the end of our trip I came across a book by Ann Armbrecht, an anthropologist who spent several months in northeastern Nepal studying the lives of the Yamphu Rai. It was a radical journey that brought her in touch with people in a vastly different culture.

Armbrecht experienced the tension between what she called the "pull of pilgrimage" and a yearning for home. After being on the road for close to a year, I could relate to what she was saying. While longing to see what lay around the next bend in the road, I also felt a tremendous urge to be back home.

Walking the tightrope between these longings, Armbrecht came in touch with "two selves," each wanting something different. "Walking alone…I felt the pull of my other self, the self who lives in the darkness in these woods…I felt that I was encountering another person—this other self of mine—the one who wants to go out and away, who longs for the wind and the rain and the wet. How to live in a way where there was room for both" (*Thin Places: A Pilgrimage Home*).

When we are pulled in different directions by expectations from outside and from within, we can be thrown completely out of whack. Like Armbrecht, we too feel the pull of the "other self" that longs for time out of the center ring of responsibility and activity. How do we make room for both the traveler and the settler? For the performer of our dreams and the one who needs to carry out daily responsibilities? For tending the household and sitting at the feet of the Master? A place to start is by looking at some common causes of an off-kilter life and how to bring ourselves into balance once again.

HONING THE SENSES

Sensory overload brought on by technology is a common reason for feeling off-balance. It no longer seems possible to get away from the constant beeping, dinging, buzzing, and pinging of electronic devices. While these tools provide enormous benefits, they also take a toll on our physical and mental well-being. "Cell phone blindness" causes people to walk straight in front of moving vehicles, while "text neck" is placing a strain on the upper back and spine. In addition to the physical danger and damage we expose ourselves to, we are also at risk of losing some vital instincts. "Nature deficit disorder," for example, is now on the official list of mental illnesses. It is caused by the incessant use of ear buds and other means of blocking out natural sounds. This, in turn, leads to a loss of the subtle senses—those instincts that warn us of danger in our natural surroundings. This is on display whenever I walk in the large national forest near our home and see runners, walkers, and hikers plugged into phones or other electronic devices. It's a pretty bad idea in a spot where one can be stalked by a mountain lion or encounter rattlesnakes and bears!

In related fashion, we seem unable to set our sights on the things that matter most. Clarence Jordan, author of the *Cotton Patch* paraphrase of the New Testament, wrote, "The reason so many people are utterly confused these days is because their eyes are not in focus. They're trying to watch too many different things and give their loyalties to too many different things." One need only watch television to see how this is true. Instead of a single image, messages scroll across the screen and commercials interrupt the flow of a program every few minutes. This leads to an overall lowering of our attention spans. We become so used to instantaneous images on our computers that we either overlook the slow growth patterns in nature or bypass them for something more engaging.

Such distractions also wear upon our spiritual senses, making prayer and reflection dry and difficult. The twelfth-century mystic Hildegard of Bingen coined the phrase "greening power" to describe the spiritual practices needed to revive a drooping soul. Even a small period spent in natural surroundings can restore a sense of balance and put us in touch with who we are and where we fit. By honing our five senses, we touch base with our physical surroundings as well as with the subtle presence of God in and around us.

Our five senses are truly amazing. Take the following facts as an example:

- The human eye can distinguish among five hundred shades of gray and spot the light of a candle fourteen miles away.

- At birth our ears are capable of discerning from among more than three hundred thousand sounds.

- The body can detect taste in as little as .0015 seconds.

- The sense of touch is the first sense developed in utero. When deprived of human touch, babies can die.

- Most people can pick up a whiff of a skunk when the amount of scent in the air is less than one ten-trillionth of an ounce.

(Jennifer Kahn, "Amazing Facts about your Senses," *Parade* magazine, July 2012)

Several years ago I started using a simple prayer of the senses to help me fall asleep when beset by worry and anxiety. I call it the FSSST prayer. It is a simple litany of the senses I used during the day: **f**eeling (touch), **s**ight, **s**ound, **s**mell, and **t**aste. The prayer not only provides a restful reflection at night but also heightens my sensate awareness throughout the day. I begin to "collect" experiences of the five senses as they happen.

The Irish author and poet John O'Donohue called the senses the "threshold of the soul" where we come to recognize God's presence both within us and around us. Honing the senses cultivates a deeper appreciation of *sacramentality*—experiencing God through what we can touch, see, hear, smell, and taste. In such a way, the FSSST prayer and other contemplative practices put us in touch with something deep inside, bringing us home to ourselves once again.

*How do you hone your senses as a way
to find better balance in your life?*

TRAVELING LIGHTLY

Jugglers know how much to handle before the balls come crashing down around them. They juggle with ease by gauging the load they can realistically handle. This makes dropping some of them a necessity. The same rings true in life. We can only keep so many balls up in the air at the same time. Even so, some of us have trouble lightening our loads. While trying to meet unrealistic expectations, we put on a false front and take on as many tasks, responsibilities, and roles as we think we can handle. When beset by a sense of over-responsibility, it can be difficult to let go of anything. This is especially true for those who care for others—parents, teachers, ministers, caregivers, and those in medical professions. Learning to lighten the load is essential in each of these roles.

While traveling across country, Ron and I chose to stay in hotels rather than a recreational vehicle for a couple of reasons. At the time, gas prices were sky-high so hotels were actually a cheaper option. We also wanted the flexibility of driving back roads that a smaller vehicle could navigate. Making our way across the country in this manner meant we couldn't pack anything extraneous. It necessitated traveling lightly.

When Jesus sent his disciples off to teach and preach, he gave them simple instructions about what to take with them: an extra pair of sandals. This served two purposes. For one, they could make a fast exit if others took exception to their preaching. For another, they had to depend on the hospitality of others in order to complete their mission.

We may have traveled with a lot more than an extra pair of shoes, but we did discover this second aspect of Jesus' traveling instructions. Our smaller mode of transportation opened us up to a tremendous amount of graciousness. On a few occasions we were hosted in the homes of friends or family. We reunited with relatives we hadn't seen in decades. Each time we were treated to sumptuous meals and rich conversation. We also enjoyed numerous encounters with people we didn't know. Hotel clerks greeted us warmly and provided directions to sites in the local area. Friendly housekeepers and restaurant servers waited on and cleaned up after us. Each experience drew us into larger circles of family and community and heightened our appreciation for the gift of hospitality.

None of us is meant to travel alone. Perhaps this is why Jesus sent the disciples out in pairs. They could share each other's joys and shoulder one another's burdens, offer encouragement and keep each other on track. Traveling in this fashion lightens the load and increases the joy of the journey.

What external or internal clutter can
you jettison in order to travel lightly?

TAMING OUR EXCESSES

The lion tamer achieves mastery over the animal by establishing himself or herself as the alpha figure. It's this bravado that enables the trainer to face down the wild beast. When the lion tamer disregards the wildness in the beast, however, the results can be catastrophic. Take, for example, the Las Vegas magicians Siegfried and Roy. While they were performing with a 350-pound Bengal tiger named Montecore, the animal suddenly sank his teeth into Roy Horn's neck and dragged him offstage. The attack left the performer partially paralyzed. The reason for the tiger's unprovoked behavior was never fully determined, but it demonstrates in tragic fashion the price of ignoring the wildness in the beast.

This is a sobering reminder about the kinds of behaviors that, when untamed, can run roughshod over our physical, mental, emotional, and spiritual well-being. Examples of these abound. Workaholism, perfectionism, the need for control, negativity, cynicism, and the quest for approval—to name a few. Each can lead to a false front that covers up deeper needs. When unchecked, we end up circling the same issues over and over again without coming to any kind of resolution.

A "wild beast" in my own life asserted itself just before we left on our trip. I was neck-deep in overseeing a conference on spirituality and mired in the details that came with it. What should have been an enlivening and creative endeavor turned into a slog when my role as chairperson morphed into several others. This was due, in part, to committee members more interested in giving advice than in doing any of the work. I was ringmaster for a circus in which most of the performers decided to sit on the sidelines! Another major factor, however, was of my own making. I tend to jump into commitments too quickly and then make them into something larger than they need to be. In this case, I opted to add a large worship component to the conference that involved substantial environmental set-up and printing of materials. I had, in effect, created a three-ring circus out of a one-act performance. Since we were in the process of moving out of our house and packing for a major trip, taking on this commitment was ill-advised at best.

During our first stop, in Santa Fe, I was still receiving emails about unpaid bills and other leftovers from the conference. It led me to consider how I get myself into such situations and what I could do to prevent them in the future. The wild beast in this case was my difficulty in saying no. There are many possible reasons for this form of excess—the quest for approval, a fear of appearing uncooperative or letting others down, the genuine interest in doing something creative without thinking the entire project through. With some time and distance, I came to the conclusion that my time on committees had come and gone; it was a center ring I no longer wanted to enter. This isn't just a case of stepping into the grandstand and letting others do all the work. Instead, I see it as a conscious decision to place my energy where I can be most open, creative, and generous while also not letting that particular beast run amuck.

In addition to our individual excesses, we have other, wilder ones with which to contend. Jesus' message is sometimes foolishly edited to exclude the warnings he gave about real and excessive dangers in the world. When we become filled with our own bravado, we are easily lulled into them. As I write this, there is an alarming rise in the level of racism, xenophobia, and scapegoating of particular groups of people. This is taking place in the United States as well as in parts of Europe, South America, Canada, Australia, and Asia. Top this off with a lust for violence and vengeance, paranoia fueled by fear or self-righteousness, and an unbridled sense of entitlement and selfishness. Jesus' call to attentiveness was not just about the small but deadly ways we can ignore the needs of our own souls but also about the toxic elements of a world that seems completely off-kilter.

In the face of such deadly excesses, it is tempting to withdraw into a center ring of our own making. There we engage with like-minded people and keep ourselves safely out of the fray. A healthy sense of self recognizes the part we play in social sin—most often through passivity and apathy. In the next chapter, we'll explore how we might allow a movement to the periphery to be one that counters toxic excesses with compassion, empathy, kindness, and generosity.

Jesus' invitation to Martha to "choose the better part" is one we should all heed. It is a call toward the edges where we can see ourselves in a more honest light. In paradoxical fashion, this is where we find our center, the place of God's "untamed grace." It is also where we may find our hearts opened in ways we have not yet imagined.

FOR REFLECTION AND DISCUSSION

Read the account of Martha and Mary (Luke 10:38–42).
How does it speak to you about spiritual balance?

Reflect on the excesses in your own life. How have you faced them
with honesty and courage? What has helped you to do this?

CHAPTER THREE

Pushed to the Periphery

A week before we left on our trip, I received a phone call from the secretary at our parish. Kay had left something for me at the office, she said. Could I come and pick it up before I left? Kay is one of those extraordinary people who continually surprise and inspire others with their thoughtfulness and generosity. I headed to the parish expecting a lovely farewell note and some little treat. What I received changed the entire journey.

Kay's gift bag contained two envelopes and a set of stretch bands (so that I could exercise along the way.) The first envelope held a twenty-dollar bill along with a card wishing us a safe and happy trip; the money was to buy snacks along the way. The other one contained twenty one-dollar bills. The accompanying note asked us to distribute the dollars to the people we encountered along the way who were in need of a cup of coffee.

Kay's dollars stretched my view of the trip far past the pretty places we would visit over the next several months. They made me attentive to those standing on street corners and along roadways asking for help and seeking a bit of human contact. As the trip lengthened, the twenty dollars morphed into something more than handouts. Long after they were gone, I continued to use our own money to extend hospitality to those beset by poverty, joblessness, mental illness, or addiction. As such, they were a reminder to make space for attentiveness and compassion.

Kay's gift also affected what I amassed along the way. After months of going through and downsizing all of our things, the last thing we needed was more stuff. So, instead of acquiring souvenirs I collected people. In addition to my journal, I kept a daily log about where we were and what we were seeing. These entries included encounters with the recipients of Kay's dollars. I also noted those following our progress through our website who were struggling with deep loss and trauma. Still others were people we met along the way:

- Two friends mourning the deaths of their beloved spouses.

- Ron's Aunt Sue who had just been moved out of her childhood home and into an assisted living center.

- The child in a neighboring hotel room whose screaming became such cause for concern that I knocked on the door to see if she was in danger.

- The woman whose barking dogs kept me awake one night. When I met her in the hotel laundry, I knew by her sad eyes that she was dealing with something far greater than unruly pets.

Each was an example of someone pushed to the periphery by physical, mental, emotional, and spiritual maladies.

We are all pushed to the periphery at one time or another. Rather than something we deny, avoid, or repress, however, such peripheral experiences can enlarge compassion toward others as well as ourselves.

What has pushed you to the periphery?

FACING OUR SHADOW

Teresa of Ávila, in her masterpiece, *The Interior Castle*, saw the soul as a mansion containing many dwellings. Spiritual growth entails moving from one to another with courage and honesty. The one dwelling in which we should always live, she wrote, is that of self-knowledge. It is akin to recognizing the faces we show others and ourselves, ones that mask our *true* selves. Through self-knowledge the performer of our dreams is less a fantasy and more of a hidden treasure waiting to be discovered.

In the previous chapter we explored what it means to tame our excesses. Part of this is acknowledging the beast within. This is what Carl Jung described as the shadow—the side of our conscious personality or persona that we seek to hide or repress. Jung used the image of a "black bag" to describe this shadow self. There we place the parts of ourselves we don't want to face—those that shame or embarrass us—as well as any flaws or failings. This has also been described as the false self or dualism—ways of taking on the performers we think we *should* be in order to meet both outer and inner expectations.

"Shadow work" isn't a spiritual self-help plan but a movement toward integration and wholeness. As Jung noted, "To round itself out, life calls not for perfection but for completeness; and for this the 'thorn in the flesh' is needed, the suffering or defects without which there is no progress and no ascent" (*Collected Works 12*).

The cliché about the clown who is laughing on the outside while crying on the inside speaks of the way in which we often try to mask the suffering that can push us to the periphery. Finding spiritual balance is not an excuse to sidestep grief, heartache, disappointment, or failure, nor is it an attempt to escape the pain of the world. If anything, it might make us more aware of it. A life of love is one of vulnerability. The gift of the clown is not disguising, denying, or suppressing the pain but allowing it to be transformed into something richer. Compassion grows through such experiences. This is the ultimate meaning of the Paschal Mystery—life emerging from the tomb, light emanating from darkness, flowers blooming in the desert. We join Jesus as a denizen of the edges where we find a vantage point for discovering the sacred in our midst.

THE TRAGIC GAP

Writer and educator Parker Palmer describes the "tragic gap" as that which lies between what is and what could be. Crossing the gap holds the tension between the primitive, reactive brain and the open, responsive heart. The latter leads to true faith and a civilized world. Such tensions give way to new thoughts, relationships, and possibilities. They provide a more expansive worldview.

What does this tension between reaction and response look like? Picture yourself on a trapeze continually swinging back and forth between what you do and what you *want* to do. Paul summed it up this way: "What I do, I do not understand. For I do not do what I want, but I do what I hate" (Romans 7:15). In other words, he *reacts* rather than *responds*.

While I was studying to be a spiritual director, I reached a major breakthrough around the tragic gap. In writing a spiritual autobiography, I began to uncover the ways in which I react to rejection (real or perceived) by withdrawing. I can trace this back to growing up in a large family in which I was the fifth of six children. By the time I was born, my older sisters were about to get married and start

families of their own. My younger brother was born three years after me. Thus, my time in the spotlight as the youngest child lasted
about five minutes. In an attempt to draw attention to myself, I used
to hide and hope that someone—particularly my mother—would
look for me. There was a major problem with this strategy, namely,
that no one knew I was hiding. As an adult I no longer seek physical hiding places but can react to perceived slights or hurt through
emotional withdrawal. In this mode I nurse my wounds and pile
up more resentment. This reaction didn't work any better in my
marriage than it did in my childhood hiding places. Take it from
me—when you are married to an introvert, the silent treatment
doesn't work!

There is a purpose to our reactions. They are a necessary part of
survival. The gap between reaction and response becomes tragic,
however, when reaction becomes our *modus operandi*. This is when,
like Paul, we end up watching ourselves do the very thing we hate
doing. We revert back to childlike patterns of behavior and make
ourselves miserable in the process.

Tara Bennett-Goleman is a psychotherapist who uses mindfulness as a way to raise awareness around the reactive brain and
the responsive heart. In her book *Emotional Alchemy,* she describes
the mental habits we form early in life that shatter our peace of
mind. She calls these *schemas*. Developed as coping mechanisms in
childhood or adolescence, many of our schemas then take root in
the brain and continue to plague us throughout our lives. Raising
awareness around them provides deeper insights into the shadow
self. This, in turn, opens possibilities for crafting compassionate responses. Bennett-Goleman's book provides an in-depth way to do
this. Common schemas include:

- **Deprivation**—the fear that our needs will never be met and
  that, no matter what we do, it isn't enough. This, in turn, leads
  to either being overly caring or overly needy.

- **Vulnerability**—the fear that we are constantly on the brink of disaster and expecting the worst to happen. Hypochondria, panic attacks, and fastidious practices hamper enjoyment of life.

- **Abandonment**—the fear that those we love the most will leave us and we'll fall apart. Reactive behaviors can range from clinging to others to circumventing possible hurt by abandoning the other person first.

- **Subjugation**—the fear of speaking up or drawing attention to oneself. Constant acquiescence to the needs and desires of others leads to pent-up resentment that can explode in over-reactive behavior or used as a way to avoid long-term commitments.

- **Mistrust**—the fear of betrayal, often as a result of childhood physical, sexual, or emotional abuse. Such a schema, developed as a protective measure, can restrict the capacity for loving relationships by raising suspicions at every turn.

- **Unlovability**—the fear of being "found out" and deemed defective. The underlying emotion is that of unworthiness, resulting in either a lack of self-confidence or an attitude of arrogance.

- **Failure**—the fear that our successes are really flukes that we don't deserve. This can lead to workaholism, perfectionism, and incessant self-abasement.

- **Entitlement**—the notion that we are owed a good life and that rules and other social conventions don't apply to us. The resultant bravado in such people often masks deep insecurity, particularly if the entitled mindset is triggered by deprivation.

- **Perfectionism**—the fear that, if we don't live up to the expectations of others, we will lose their love. Like those driven by deprivation or failure, we are driven to overactivity or hyper-responsibility by a deep sense of inadequacy.

- **Exclusion**—the fear that we are missing out on something and constantly on the outside of social circles and acceptability. We might react by keeping ourselves on the outer circles or by glorying in the role of the outsider.

Like the wild beasts that run amuck, we "tame" these schemas not through bravado and false fronts but by paying attention to them. Learning to identify and then face our reactive selves in order to develop compassionate responses takes time and intention. Bennett-Goleman, a practicing Buddhist, uses meditation* to help her patients traverse the tragic gap.

Becoming mindful of our reactive modes and the schemas that drive them is a part of the self-knowledge that Teresa of Ávila extols in *The Interior Castle*. Such knowledge also forms part of spiritual practices like the Examen*—a five-step reflection that draws us into deeper awareness of our emotions and the presence of God in our lives.

*Which of these schemas resonates in your life?
How has it resulted in reactive behavior?*

FROM REACTION TO RESPONSE

Reading Bennett-Goleman's description of schemas was a major spiritual breakthrough for me. It not only shed light on some of my own reactive behavior but also broadened an understanding of sin as something that sets us off-kilter by disrupting relationships with others, ourselves, and God. It also explains why some of my best-intentioned efforts at reversing behaviors so often failed. Like many cradle Catholics of my generation, I learned that if I simply confessed my bad behavior and then made a mental resolution to refrain from repeating it, I would have a handle on it. I soon learned that trying to tame my excesses through willpower wasn't enough.

In truth, the theology around sin and reconciliation runs much deeper than thinking ourselves into right behavior. There is a need for conversion, which is a matter of the heart. The self-knowledge that Teresa of Ávila and other spiritual mystics embrace is not perpetual navel-gazing or a journey into narcissism. Instead, it is a humble way to face who we are—"warts and all." Rather than engaging in "spiritual make-overs" through trying to cage the wild beasts, we pay attention to them. We listen to and learn what they have to teach us about ourselves and about the capacity for enlarging our hearts through compassionate responses. It's about *willingness* rather than *willfulness*. Taking the schemas one by one, we can see how one might move from the reactive brain to the responsive heart:

- **Deprivation**. By resisting the temptation to think about what is lacking in our lives, we can respond by cultivating gratitude and considering what we might offer to others.

- **Vulnerability**. Centering ourselves through breathing* and clearing the mind of anxiety and worry is a way to tamp down the panic. It also allows room for a more expansive worldview.

- **Abandonment**. Dealing with this schema requires a building up of trust in oneself, in others, and in God. Recalling times in which someone has left and life didn't fall apart places life in perspective and gives us the courage to move forward.

- **Subjugation**. Letting feelings of resentment rise may feel threatening at first, but paying attention to such emotions affords an insight into their origins. By getting in touch with the experiences in which we have felt dominated or undermined by others, we build self-confidence grounded in an understanding of God's infinite mercy and love. Journaling* is one helpful way to do this.

- **Mistrust**. Those who have experienced abuse may need the help of a professional therapist, counselor, or spiritual director who will help to rebuild a sense of personal safety and, in time, an ability to regard others with an openness of heart while also maintaining healthy boundaries.

- **Unlovability**. Naming and harnessing the inner critic is a step towards seeing oneself as loving and lovable. Psalm 139 is a wonderful expression of the love God has for each of us, one perfect for reflection through *Lectio Divina**.

- **Failure**. Few of our great saints were models of success. Reading their stories and those of others who learned more from their failures than their successes can help put the inner critic to rest and provide a broader perspective.

- **Entitlement**. Teresa of Ávila favored humility above all other virtues. A conscious reflection on a humble recognition that I am no better or worse than anyone else puts the ego in check and allows the true self to emerge.

- **Perfectionism**. By consciously untangling worthiness and lovability from perfection, we let go of unrealistic expectations of ourselves and learn to go with the flow of life. In the meantime, the lessening of perfection-oriented behavior allows more time for taking care of our true needs.

- **Exclusion.** Paying attention to tendencies toward self-pity or to shielding ourselves from hurt by setting ourselves apart is the first step in recognizing how this schema comes into play. We can then make an intentional effort to connect with someone else and experience the joy that comes with it. This is the response I have been trying to make when tempted to revert to my reactive mode of withdrawal.

In his Second Letter to the Corinthians, Paul lamented the "thorn in the flesh" that upset the balance of faith and devotion he wanted to give to God and to others. He not only came to recognize that the thorn wasn't going to be magically removed but also that it held transformative potential. "Therefore, I am content with weaknesses, insults, hardships, persecutions, and constraints, for the sake of Christ; for when I am weak, then I am strong" (2 Corinthians 12:10). The push to the periphery opens us up to this paradoxical experience of grace embedded in the wound.

TRAVERSING THE TRAGIC GAP

The intersection between psychology and spirituality is intriguing. Bennett-Golemen's approach is one example of this. I wonder how Teresa, for her part, might have applied the valuable insights of human psychology to her description of the interior castle. While psychological understanding leads us to a recognition of our schemas and where they originated, spiritual work helps us learn how something hopeful can arise from them.

Parker Palmer points out that every religious tradition has some kind of belief in the alchemy that can transform suffering into something life-giving. In the Christian tradition, the Easter hope of the resurrection of Christ doesn't come without an immersion into the Good Friday experience of the cross. The process of recognizing and owning our shadow side is not easy and sometimes not very pleasant. It takes a willingness to open the heart and then to have it broken. This happens in one of two ways.

The first is the heart shattered. We then take the shards of our brokenness and aim them at others. "Here the heart is an unresolved wound that we carry with us for a long time, sometimes tucking it away and feeding it as a hidden wound, sometimes trying to 'resolve it' by inflicting the same wound on others" (Parker Palmer, "The Broken-open Heart: Living with Faith and Hope in the Tragic Gap," *Weavings*, Volume XXIV, No. 2). If you have ever been the target of someone's shattered heart, you know it is a painful and sometimes dangerous place to be.

This is true not only for individuals but also for communities. As a resident of Colorado, I have witnessed the aftermath of two mass shootings—one at Columbine High School and the other at a movie theater in Aurora. After the initial shock waves subsided, the reactions set in. Heartbreak gave rise to blaming others for allowing such horrific things to happen—civic and educational institutions, the school principal and owner of the movie theater, parents, therapists and counselors, the gun lobby and the anti-gun lobby, and so forth. Fear set off reactive ideas and "solutions"—more guns and guards, more suspicion and scapegoating, more programs, laws, and metal detectors. I am not saying some of these measures are not without merit, but the lack of thoughtful responses in such situations shows how shattered hearts can result in wounds that affect a community for decades.

The other form of heartbreak is the experience of being broken *open*. This enlarges the capacity for empathy and attendance to the suffering of others. It is the essence of compassion. Kay, the parishioner whose dollars widened the scope of our trip, exemplifies someone with a broken-open heart. In addition to a number of physical ailments, she has also known terrible grief. At the time of our trip, she and her husband were mourning the death of their daughter and raising the two adolescent children she left behind. Ron and I were the last people Kay should have had time for. Instead, her generous heart not only considered our well-being but also those whom she had never even met. Her open-heartedness reminds me of all that keeps us human, alive, caring, and compassionate in the way of Jesus.

Palmer names three ways across the tragic gap toward open-hearted response. The first is *acknowledging and naming our suffering* rather than trying to suppress, deny, or rationalize it. This entails stepping outside of the false expectations put upon us by others as well as ourselves. It can be especially dodgy for those who take on the role of the strong man/woman. Coming to grips with our own areas of weakness and vulnerability requires a different kind of strength. To do this, we need travel companions who are trustworthy and willing to listen rather than those who ply us with platitudes or pile on the advice. Paying attention to our emotions and reactions leads us to recognize the schemas behind them and offers an entry into open-hearted responses.

The second way is *moving directly to the heart of the pain, allowing ourselves to feel it rather than numb it*. We live in a culture that consistently denies death and seeks ever-increasing ways to escape hurt and discomfort through an overdose of substances or activity. As Palmer notes, "The only way to transform suffering into something life-giving is to enter into it so deeply that we learn what it has to teach us and come out on the other side." It is easy to slip into the role of the clown by making light of our own struggles rather than acknowledging how real they are. Living out of a responsive heart attunes us to the need for honesty without succumbing to the reactive stance of perpetual victimhood or morbid obsession with our own problems.

The third way is *creating a space of quiet around us so that the turmoil can settle and an inner peace can emerge.* This kind of space is not found in center ring. Those drawn to the role of the ringmaster find it particularly hard to exit the epicenter of activity and distraction in favor of the silence* and solitude* of the periphery. Nevertheless, these two spiritual practices are essential for coming in touch with our true identity and needs. Jesus as the model Sabbath keeper illustrates the value of stepping out on a regular basis. In the gospels we see him gravitating toward deserted places in order to pray, fast, and recollect himself. He then moves back into the center of his ministry with a deepened capacity for compassion and attentiveness to others.

REIGNITING COMPASSION

When mapping out our route, Ron and I didn't seek out the most depressing places we could find. I don't suppose that's the goal of many travelers. Instead we sought places of beauty and peace, ones where we felt safe and welcome. Even so, Kay's dollars ignited our sense of compassion while traversing the vast landscape of this country. The money opened a door to conversation with people we might have otherwise bypassed.

In her article "Sensing Compassion," Regina Bechtle, SC, describes how the use of her five senses reignites compassion when she is feeling "prickly" and inwardly focused. "Without fail, my senses open the door to an expanding room where I am connected with God and all that God loves" (*Weavings*, Volume XXXI, No. 2). This puts a new spin on the FSSST prayer. Rather than centering exclusively on sensations that are pleasing and gratifying, we open our hearts to a more merciful and incarnational view of the world around us. Our senses awaken to those pushed to the periphery as well as those who care for them. Here is how this might unfold:

> The *feeling* that comes when offered a healing or loving touch
> brings to mind the compassionate outreach of those who tend

the wounds of others—both physically and spiritually. One of
the most devastating aspects of being on the margins of society,
such as those imprisoned or homeless, is the lack of human touch.
Awakening this sense reignites compassion toward those deprived
of this vital act of caring.

The *sight* of someone standing on a street corner, asking not
only for a dollar to assuage their hunger but also for an acknowl-
edgment of his or her humanity, can evoke empathy and understanding. Awakening this sense keeps us from turning away from
people or events that disturb or challenge us. When offering one
of Kay's dollars to another, I tried to look them in the eye—a
simple yet vital form of human contact.

The *sound* of weeping and lament among those struck down by
grief, loss, disappointment, and failure can remind us of the power
of presence during times of desolation. Awakening to this brings
a certain comfort level with tears or expressions of anguish, anger,
grief, and pain. Like Bechtle, I am also a spiritual director. This
role calls for listening attentively to stories of suffering, confusion,
and despair that sometimes leave me drained. Even so, I am also
aware of their sacred nature and how important it is to hold each
story with care and humility.

The *smell* of unpleasantness—"the rank odor of garbage on hot
city streets or the stink of urine in a corner of a train station"
(Bechtle)—can reignite compassion in a visceral way. I recall
being in a coffee shop with a women's spirituality group on a cold
Colorado day when a homeless man entered seeking warmth. His
pungent odor filled the room and made it hard to maintain our
conversation. Trying to remain present to him with compassion
was both a challenge and a grace-filled reminder of all the ameni-
ties of a home that we easily take for granted.

The *taste* of good food reminds Bechtle of the many people who labor to bring it to her table as well as to consider the millions of people who know hunger because of natural disasters and human-caused crises. This isn't meant to be a self-induced guilt trip, however. Using our sense of taste to awaken compassion can draw us more fully into savoring the goodness of God's gifts while also motivating us to help those in need.

This reflective use of the senses is a simple way to develop *incarnational awareness*—recognition of God's presence in all that we touch, see, hear, smell, and taste. God is with us in our sickness and our health, in the times of joy and of sorrow, in the ordinary and extraordinary moments of our lives. Incarnational awareness draws us out of the center ring of self-absorption and fixation on our small circle of concerns. It opens up a vast and colorful worldview in which we see how we are part of the whole circus instead of a solo act. It is an avenue into love.

In his book *The Awakened Heart*, the late Gerald May describes love as a *capacity* rather than a function. Capacity implies space; it refers to how much we can potentially hold. "It is out of the pristine ground of the heart that true assent and fidelity must finally come, stripped of external justifications and rational explanation." If there is one single key to a life of spiritual balance it's the one that opens the heart—to ourselves, to others, to God. Incarnational awareness strips off the masks we place on ourselves or others. It replaces an opaque way of seeing with transparent vision—seeing others as God sees them. Kay's dollars transformed my own vision, not only for a trip across the country, but also for a broader spiritual journey.

FOR REFLECTION AND DISCUSSION

What compassionate responses can you craft to counter your schemas and make your way across the tragic gap?

How might you reignite compassion through the use of your five senses?

CHAPTER FOUR

Pitching a Tent

WHEN THE CIRCUS COMES TO TOWN, IT PITCHES A TENT—A TEMPORARY PLACE FOR THE ACTS AND ACTIVITIES THAT FOLLOW. The "big top" remains an enduring symbol as a place to move out of the mainstream and gather together with others for entertainment and enjoyment.

Growing up as I did in Colorado, I am used to the sight of campers taking off for the mountains. They head to peripheral places to pitch tents in order to exit urban life and center themselves in the natural world. I have never been a camper. The closest I came to sleeping outdoors was a miserable childhood experience in a sleeping bag on a playmate's back porch. This aversion to roughing it was another reason Ron and I chose hotels over campgrounds for our trip. Even so, our experience of moving across the country was not unlike campers seeking respite from center ring and finding temporary quarters along the way.

My journal reflected the transient nature of our travels. "Home,"

I wrote in one entry, "is wherever we pitch our tent." We were indeed making a home wherever we went, and I had a clear sense that God was moving right along with us. This recognition continued to diminish those first-night fears about what could go wrong. I slowly began to appreciate all that could go *right*. This, in turn, led to deeper realizations about the importance of life on the road.

TEMPORARY DWELLINGS

The Jewish celebration of the Feast of Tabernacles is a nine-day harvest festival that takes place in the fall. Part of the ritual involves the construction of a temporary hut called a *sukkot* where family and friends gather to eat, drink, and sing together. This follows the injunction in Leviticus 23:42–43: "You shall dwell in booths for seven days; every native-born Israelite shall dwell in booths, that your descendants may realize that, when I led the Israelites out of the land of Egypt, I made them dwell in booths. I, the LORD, am your God." The fragility of the temporary structure is a reminder of the human need for God.

The structure of the sukkot has certain specifications. It must consist of at least two and one-half walls so one can see one's neighbor. It should be built with material sturdy enough to withstand the natural elements. The roof must be made of something that grows from the ground and allows a view of the sun and stars. In his book *Common Prayers*, Harvey Cox explains the significance of this little shelter. It serves as a reminder that we can never entirely shield ourselves from the threats to our lives and well-being. We must ultimately rely on God. "It also reminds us that even within this fragile shanty, and exposed to all the vicissitudes of life, we can still eat and drink and enjoy friends and family."

David Steindl-Rast names two opposing tendencies that break the rules of the sukkot structure. One is the tendency to **drift**. The perpetual wanderer cannot build and lacks the rootedness one needs to be stable and well-grounded. The circus life might be an itinerant one, but it isn't without a sense of direction. Once stakes are pulled up it moves to the next destination on its itinerary. Circuses also tend to follow the seasons and thus take time off when road conditions make it too risky or unprofitable to travel.

It is not uncommon today to find spiritual seekers adrift in a sea of options. They dip their toe into classic spiritualities, such as Christian mysticism or Buddhist meditation, before moving on to something else. Building a spiritual practice takes time and intention. It requires growth and stabilizing forces such as community, discipline, ritual, and trustworthy guides.

Perpetual discontent is another form of drifting. When we are constantly on the lookout for the next best gadget, ideal job, or perfect relationship, we are in perpetual motion. After a while, spiritual ennui sets in, and cynicism, depression, and resentment take hold. Sometimes the discontent is with ourselves. Rather than doing the long and sometimes difficult spiritual work necessary for growth, we look for quick fixes and surface solutions.

The other tendency is to **entrench**. We build our structure and then resist leaving it to explore a wider world and a broader understanding of life. The walls of our tents harden into stone and we are no longer able to glimpse the neighbor next store or the stars above. The need for security and safety drives all else, restricting the capacity for joy, wonder, and a spirit of adventure. Ironically, a tendency to entrench can be triggered by the plethora of choices we now have—from things as mundane as a multiple brands of toothpaste to serious decisions about careers or relationships. This, in turn, can lead to a paralysis called "future regret"—the inability to act based on a fear of making the wrong choice.

There are other forms of fear that engender entrenchment. Even if we are miserable, stepping into something new can be daunting and overwhelming. Boredom and apathy arise as we grow used to the idea that nothing will ever change. I once heard someone describe it this way: It's not that life is one damn thing after another, but the same damn thing over and over again. Self-defeating thoughts and behaviors prevent us from expanding our vision or imagining greater possibilities for ourselves or for the world. Entrenchment can be a huge problem in institutions as well as individuals. Consider political or educational systems bogged down by established ways of operating or decision making. Religious institutions become so focused on enforcing rules and worshiping dogma—which the late Edward Hays called "beliefs set in stone"— that they lose touch with their basic mission. This makes Pope Francis's description of the church as a "field hospital" all the more intriguing. It's not only an image that implies flexibility and the ability to move with the needs of those it tends, but it also speaks to the importance of caring for those pushed to the periphery by suffering. Compassion, empathy, and hospitality all become the "walls" of an institution ready to minister to those on the margins.

Which tendency do you lean toward—drifting or entrenching? How can you pitch a tent that finds a balance between them?

There are various ways tent pitching can restore spiritual balance. Here are some I find particularly helpful.

SEEKING SMALL SPACES
Another aspect of the tent is its small size. Even the "big top," while large enough to hold a crowd, has manageable dimensions that allow the audience to view the entire panorama of performers.

Despite my aversion to pitching a tent in the wilderness, I have always been taken with small spaces. As a child, I sought out the many nooks and crannies in our large family home in which to snuggle down to read, play, think, or dream. Thus, when Ron and I discovered a delightfully different small space in the course of our travels, we couldn't resist. Treehouse Point is located just outside of Seattle and offers individual lodgings in the large trees on the property. A central house provides additional rooming options, daily breakfast, and access to full bathrooms. Our tree house was perched forty feet above a small river and was accessed by a suspension bridge. A skylight over the bed provided light in the day and met one of the loveliest requirements of a sukkot at night—a view of the stars. Once we hunkered down inside of it, we were loath to leave. Entrenchment could have easily become a way of life!

My favorite of the Christian mystics is a woman who found another small space in which to pitch a tent. Julian of Norwich was an *anchoress*—someone who moves to the periphery in a radical way. The word comes from a Greek root meaning to retire. The earliest Christian anchorites went to the desert for sustained prayer and meditation. By the fifteenth century, the practice was not as extreme. Instead of heading to the wilderness, anchorites and anchoresses enclosed themselves in small cells, often built up against the wall of a church. This radical step out of ordinary life was a death of sorts. It was thus ritualized with the reception of "last rites" and then a sealing into the cell through a vow to remain there until death.

Julian (whose real identity is not known; her name is most likely taken from the church of Saint Julian to which her cell was attached) lived a simple but not particularly austere life as an anchoress. She had a housekeeper who cooked and cleaned for her as well as access to the church and its gardens. There were two windows—or "squints"—in Julian's cell. One allowed her to participate in church services. The other opened to the street where she could offer spiritual counsel to visitors from the outside world. The squints made her a hermit but not a solitary; she had contact with other people rather than living in complete isolation.

Julian is credited as the first woman to write a book in English.

While she gave it no title, it is known to us today as *The Showings of Julian of Norwich*—a magnificent recounting of the mystical visions she was given. She recorded these "showings" in her small space away from the center of world events. Even there she could hone her subtle senses by recognizing the generosity of God in the limited number of material goods surrounding her. This is evident in her reflection on an object she described as "small as a hazelnut." "It lasts and always will, because God loves it; and thus everything has being through the love of God. In this little thing I saw three properties. The first is that God made it, the second is that God loves it, and the third is that God preserves it" (*Showings*, Fifth Chapter). When something as humble as a hazelnut can draw out such incarnational awareness, the possibilities for perceiving God's gifts in small spaces become endless.

What small spaces bring a deeper recognition of God's presence in your life?

The small space to which Julian withdrew gave way to an expansion of yet another: her own heart. The heart as a locus for the indwelling presence of God is a concept stretching way back in time. There are over one thousand references to it in the Bible—more than those referring to the body, mind, or even the soul. "For the ancient Hebrews," says writer Gail Godwin, "heart, *lev*, meant the seat of wisdom and understanding, the inner personality, the whole gamut of emotional life, as well as the collective mind, or mind-set, of the people, the mental heart as well as the fleshy heart ..." (*Heart: A Natural History of the Heart-filled Life*).

In Jesus' teaching about prayer, the room he tells his disciples to enter (Matthew 6:6) is not a physical space. After all, the houses of that time were primarily communal places; this made the notion of one's own room an anomaly. Rather, the secret place known only to God is the heart. Gerald May describes it as "the place where we are in most intimate contact with God's presence and with our essential union with others, where the deep, ongoing love affair between God and human beings actually takes place" (*The Awakened Heart*). It is here where we find ourselves capable, like Julian, of recognizing God's gifts of mercy and love in things as small as a hazelnut.

FINDING GOD IN THE DETAILS
Midway through our trip, I received an invitation from an Episcopal women's group to direct a retreat upon our return to Colorado. Through one of their members, they learned of our journey and were intrigued. "Could you center the retreat on the images of God you are discovering as you travel?" they asked. It was another out-of-the-blue experience that, like Kay's dollars, altered my view of the road. I began to look more closely at all we were seeing, particularly through Ron's photographic lens.

It wasn't hard to sight the grandeur of God in places like the Grand Canyon, the giant redwoods forest, or the edge of the oceans on either side of the country. The retreat invitation prompted me to pay closer attention to the presence of the Divine in the details as well, such as the delicate patterns of sand newly swept by a wave or the intricacies of a spider web backlit by the sun. Some experiences were opened to us by others. My cousin in St. Louis gave us tickets to the Missouri Botanical Gardens, where we spent a lovely afternoon amid a gorgeous array of flowers as well as an impressive display of mosaic sculptures. Our children joined us for Christmas in Clearwater, Florida. We ended up, at our daughter's prodding, swimming with giant manatees as part of a guided excursion. Each experience underscored the importance of stepping out each day with receptivity to surprise. Pitching a tent with a window open to both the vastness of the world as well as its intricacies is a natural step toward a contemplative vision.

Wilki Au describes this vision in his book, *Spirituality for the Long Haul*. "Contemplation," he writes, "enriches our spirituality by extending our awareness of God beyond specific times set aside for formal prayer. It deepens our capacity to find God in all things." Poet Elizabeth Barrett Browning put it another way:

Earth's crammed with heaven
And every common bush afire with God,
But only he who sees takes off his shoes;
The rest sit round and pluck blackberries.

Someone who seemed to recognize the extraordinary in the ordinary was Percy Ainsworth, a Methodist minister who died of typhoid fever in 1909, at the age of thirty-six. One of his friends remembered him as a talented preacher who opened people to "the mystery of the soul's life." His writing attests to this. Working with a single verse from a psalm or an image from a gospel account, he had a gift for drawing out insights that would sail past most of us. It's fascinating to read how he described the early part of the twentieth century as one in which people seemed to be rushing around in a frenzy of busyness. I wonder what he would make of today's high-tech world.

Ainsworth readily acknowledged that we can't ignore the rush of life but that we can strive to follow the example of the "quietness" of Jesus. This was possible, he noted, because Jesus lived for the essential things. Without this, life remains a three-ring circus with simultaneous activities all vying for our attention. "The world is in a mighty hurry, not because life is so full…but because it is so empty; not because it touches reality at so many points, but because it misses it at all points. The more we hurry the less we live" ("Faith and Haste," *Weavings*, Volume XVIII, No. 1). The wish for more time is, in reality, a longing for more eternity—something we find off-road and in the midst of the small details that are woven into the fabric of life. Even then, it takes intention to step away from the things that pull us in different directions in order to discover the fullness of life.

STEPPING OUT

We may not be able to escape the rush of life but we can counter the toll it takes by sharpening our contemplative vision. As I noted in Chapter 1, the decision to exit center ring requires taking the first—and hardest—step. Stepping out was the way Ron and I not only started the journey, but also stayed engaged with it.

After about three months, our time on the road began to feel like the new normal. As such, there was the possibility of succumbing to inertia. Stepping out was a constant challenge, particularly in places where we didn't think there was much to see. One of these was Burley, Idaho. After a long day's drive, we were tempted to entrench by hanging around our hotel room to watch reruns on TV. Resisting this urge, we pulled out a guide to Idaho's state parks and made our way to Shoshone Falls. Finding this spectacular sight (at 212 feet, the falls are higher than Niagara Falls) in a place where we had no expectations reinvigorated us and reengaged us with our travels. It also reminded us of the importance of stepping out anew each day. This was particularly true when the routine was wearing thin or we were in danger of burnout and boredom. Stepping out not only provided a fresh view of our surroundings but also served to recommit us to the journey. So it is with spiritual practice.

What tempts you to disengage from daily routines
and responsibilities? How might you step out
in order to reengage with life?

Consider the perils a circus performer faces when he steps onto the tightrope or into a cage with a wild animal. What gives the trapeze artist the courage to let go of the bar and trust that her partner will be there to catch her? The spiritual journey entails a certain level of risk. We leave behind what we know as familiar and venture into the unknown. Remember how Jesus called his disciples? With three simple words—"Come, follow me"—he drew them out of their comfort zones. They left behind jobs, possessions, and even their families. Jesus was not asking them to be irresponsible vagabonds, however. Instead, he challenged them to step out into new territory, to see the world and God's working in it with new eyes and expanded hearts.

This is not a process, of course, just for the road, but for everyday life. In the Sermon on the Mount Jesus spoke powerfully about God's abundant care for us and the importance of stepping out each day in trust.

> Therefore I tell you, do not worry about your life, what you will eat [or drink], or about your body, what you will wear. Is not life more than food and the body more than clothing? Look at the birds in the sky; they do not sow or reap, they gather nothing into barns, yet your heavenly Father feeds them. Are not you more important than they? Can any of you by worrying add a single moment to your life-span? Why are you anxious about clothes? Learn from the way the wild flowers grow. They do not work or spin. But I tell you that not even Solomon in all his splendor was clothed like one of them. If God so clothes the grass of the field, which grows today and is thrown into the oven tomorrow, will he not much more provide for you, O you of little faith? So do not worry and say, "What are we to eat?" or "What are we to drink?" or "What are we to wear?" All these things the pagans seek. Your heavenly Father knows that you need them all. But seek first the kingdom [of God] and his righteousness, and all these things will be given you besides. Do not worry about tomorrow; tomorrow will take care of itself. (Matthew 6:25–34)

This passage has a special place in our lives because Ron and I chose it as the gospel for our wedding. In the forty years since that memorable day the importance of letting go has resonated strongly in our lives. Perhaps that's what enabled us to take the first step into a yearlong journey on the road. Despite my initial anxieties, the road opened up before us. It not only brought new experiences but also a new way of seeing. Worrying about what might lie around the next bend generates myopic vision and shuts down possibility. Pitching a tent in the world does the opposite. Even so, we are not going to get very far without discipline.

PRACTICING SPIRITUAL DISCIPLINE

One of the most fascinating aspects of the circus is the seeming ease with which each performer carries out her or his task. As with any talent it doesn't come without practice and the honing of skill. A certain amount of entrenchment is needed to obtain the proficiency of a master circus performer. It takes discipline to reach this stage.

The same holds true for the spiritual life. Discipline keeps us on the right path and involves concentration, dedication, and intent. It also requires a taming of our wild instincts and desires. The word itself is derived from the same root word as disciple. To be a disciple of anything—music, art, sports—takes discipline. What, then, does it mean to practice discipline as a means toward spiritual balance?

In Buddhist practice, discipline is a way to focus on the present moment. Pema Chodron, a Buddhist nun and author, describes what this means. "What we discipline is not our 'badness' or our 'wrongness.' What we discipline is any form of potential escape from reality. ... Discipline allows us to be right here and connect with the richness of the moment ... [The] journey of discipline provides the encouragement that allows us to let go. It's a sort of undoing process that supports us in going against the grain of our painful habitual patterns" (*When Things Fall Apart*).

This approach underscores the work of identifying our schemas and crafting new responses. Lest we think this isn't a challenge for those who enter the contemplative life, one only need look at how some of our great saints and mystics struggled with it. Thomas Merton, for example, walked the tightrope between his desire for solitude and his place in the monastic community, with his longing to retreat from the world and his drive to be part of it through his writing. The hermitage that he built at the monastery at Gethsemani was a way of pitching a tent in order to keep these tensions in balance. It provided him a temporary space apart from the rest of the community where he further developed a practice of contemplative prayer and a mindful way of living.

In spiritual direction, one of the most frequent laments I hear involves a lack of discipline. It ranges from the frustration of well-intended efforts at contemplation and prayer getting sidelined by activity (Martha overtaking Mary, so to speak) to the distracted "monkey mind" that keeps one from being present to the moment. I also find people trying to take on a discipline that isn't well-suited to their temperaments or circumstances. It's like trying to take on the role of a circus performer for which you have no context or training. This is when spiritual drifting can throw us off-kilter. I recall the advice a friend once received from a wizened spiritual guide. When she confessed to her frustration at not being able to practice centering prayer,* due to lack of time and a houseful of small children, he told her, "Don't pray what you can't; pray what you can."

CULTIVATING MINDFULNESS

Ron and I started our trip in February 2008. I noted earlier what a tumultuous time this was for the country and the world. As the political and economic news grew more dismal we continued to travel in relative oblivion, sometimes by opting out of the news in favor of remaining present to the journey. One of the most ironic moments came when we ended up at Walden Pond on the same day that the global financial firm, Lehman Brothers, declared bankruptcy.

Henry David Thoreau's experience of Walden Woods and the chronicle of his discoveries is a classic example of exiting center ring. His house is long gone but its outlines are still marked with cornerstones. Its small size is an apt illustration of his desire for an uncluttered life. Walking around the pond (which is actually a good-sized lake) puts one in touch with the love Thoreau had for such a beautiful yet simple place. It is easy to understand his endless fascination with nature and the pleasure of traversing a well-trod path where the abundance of nature was on full display. Thoreau considered an immersion into the natural elements as essential to living a full life. "We need the tonic of wildness—to wade sometimes in the marshes where the bittern and the meadow-hen lurk, and hear the booming of the snipe; to smell the whispering sedge where only some wilder and more solitary fowl builds her nest, and the mink crawls with its belly close to the ground" (*Walden*). These are not observations taken from a casual stroll or a jaunt through the woods while plugged into an iPod. Thoreau made a conscious choice to go to the woods of Walden "because I wished to live deliberately, to front only the essential facts of life, and see if I could not learn what it had to teach, and not, when I came to die, discover that I had not lived." His words convey something akin to Percy Ainsworth's observation that "faith in Jesus Christ teaches us that every person must have time to live."

The image of God as immanent is one awash in details. We can easily miss traces of the Divine if we live mindlessly. Common bushes are afire with God if we take time to look and see. Contemplative vision awakens us to the recognition that God is closer than we think. Traditional images of contemplation often place it outside of everyday existence, such as a monastery or a Walden Pond. Most of us, however, find it in ordinary life. All that is required is remaining alert and attentive. Thus, Jesus' call to observe the lilies of the field and the birds of the air is not just a means of releasing anxiety but also a way to recognize the face of God in the smallest details. Thomas Merton described contemplation as spiritual wonder and open-mouthed awe at the pure sanctity of being alive. "It is a vivid realization of the fact that life and being in us proceed from an invisible, transcendent and infinitely abundant Source. Contemplation is, above all, awareness of the reality of that Source. It *knows* the Source, obscurely, inexplicably, but with a certitude that goes both beyond reason and beyond simple faith" (*New Seeds of Contemplation*). Such vision inevitably moves us to a place of gratefulness.

NURTURING GRATITUDE

When Ron and I reached Michigan, we took a day trip to Mackinac Island—a lovely out-of-center-ring spot devoid of cars and dependent on bicycles and horse-drawn carts for transportation. On the drive back to our hotel we passed through the town of Charlevoix where a five-mile stretch of road was planted with brilliantly colored petunias, something we came to learn is an annual custom of the local residents. Later we meandered off the highway and came across a field of bright yellow sunflowers. It was a day that unfolded in a cascade of surprise—the key to unlocking a grateful heart.

David Steindl-Rast describes surprise as the seed of gratitude. "To recognize that everything is surprising is the first step toward recognizing that everything is gift" (*Gratefulness, the Heart of Prayer*). Surprises differ from rude awakenings. These jolt us into reality when we discover the truth that we did not expect. We are then set off balance by disappointment, anger, pessimism, or fear. Surprise, on the other hand, keeps us on our toes, ready to step out each day with the heart of an adventurer and the grace of the most practiced circus performer.

This is not to say that every surprise is as lovely as a road lined with petunias or a field full of sunflowers. Some surprises are unwelcome and unwarranted. This makes hope the tightrope strung between what Steindl-Rast describes as the "already and the not-yet." It's not hard to find the surprise in a plethora of colorful flowers; the recognition of grace is immediate. Other gifts take time to unwrap. Calamitous episodes can catch us by surprise and throw us into a whirl of confusion, grief, anxiety, or dread. With time, patience, and trust in a longer view of life, the grace emerges, and a different kind of surprise takes hold.

Meister Eckhart, the great German theologian and mystic, famously wrote that if the only prayer we uttered during the course of the day was "thank you," that would be enough. The gift of gratitude awakens us to a "just enough" view of life—one of contentment and joy. Discontented people rarely express gratitude for what they have; instead they focus on what they lack. This rings true not only in terms of physical possessions but also in personal traits. When we find ourselves set off-kilter over the kind of performer we think we should be, we are ensnared by perpetual dissatisfaction over who we are and what we do. This leads to an obsession over what is lacking in ourselves and in our lives.

I wonder if this wasn't what Julian experienced in the confines of her church cell. The world outside her window was certainly not idyllic. The Black Plague was devastating Europe, crop failures were threatening famine, and England was mired in the Hundred Years War with France. She was visited by people seeking comfort, consolation, inspiration, and advice. It probably wore her down, and she must have heard stories that broke her heart. While she is best known for her famous quote, "All will be well, and all will be well, and all manner of things will be well," she also observed how our lives are a mixture of both wellness and woe. Her ability to find wonder and the grace of God in an object as small as a hazelnut attests to her open and grateful heart.

One way to counter self-obsessive thoughts is by focusing on all that is plentiful in our lives. Sarah Ban Breathnach, author of

Simple Abundance, urges a consideration of what we have rather than what we lack. Doing so reveals the great profusion of grace that surrounds us but that, through myopic vision, we tend to miss. Several years ago a group of friends gave me a journal based on Breathnach's writings on gratitude. It had just enough space each day to write one line about something for which I was thankful. Since I already kept a regular journal I didn't expect to make much use of it. Even so, I decided to use it as an Advent practice. It was so inspiring that I kept going until I had cycled through the entire year. The little journal turned out to be a lifesaver. The year unfolded in a series of rude awakenings over a job that didn't suit me and the aftermath of a traumatic loss in our family. Setting aside a moment each day to record something for which I was grateful realigned my thinking and prodded me to look beyond disappointment, anxiety, and dread. I discovered what Breathnach meant about gratitude holding us together even when we are falling apart. "Ironically," she says, "gratitude's most powerful mysteries are often revealed when we are struggling in the midst of personal turmoil. When we stumble in the darkness, rage in anger, hurl faith across the room, abandon all hope. While we cry ourselves to sleep, gratitude waits patiently to console and reassure us; there is a landscape larger than the one we can see" (*The Simple Abundance Journal of Gratitude*).

Five years after completing the journal, I reread the entries and tracked with one each day over the course of a year. I made new entries in the margins as I went, often in connection with my original ones. At the end of this second round of practice, I wrote the following: "I still find it stunning to read over these entries and how much we came through in one year. If the year was a challenge, it was also a tremendous blessing. Things unfolded in ways we could not have foreseen. Thus, I am ever grateful for another grace-filled year." In short, I was taken by surprise at how the daily practice of gratitude not only revealed the way in which God was with me through a trying time; it also heightened my awareness of the richness of my life, one contemplated most fully within the quieting of body, mind, heart, and soul.

When have you been taken by surprise that opened into gratitude, perhaps in an unexpected way?

SAVORING SILENCE AND SOLITUDE

After being pushed to the periphery by her own grief and that of a friend, Anne D. LeClaire embarked on a different kind of journey—one that led to sustained periods of silence.* It started out as a commitment to not speaking for a full twenty-four hours. Discovering the difference between periods of "accidental" silence and intentional ones led her out of the center ring of distraction and busyness to a place of inner quiet and calm. For over twenty years she has maintained a practice of total silence on the first and third Mondays of the month. This, in turn, brought her to a place of solitude* in which time slowed and she reconnected with something vital in herself. "Alone, with my thoughts for company, I befriended my private self, all of me, my weaknesses and my fundamental worthiness. That was the challenge and the reward of my alone time" (*Listening Below the Noise*).

LeClaire was tapping into something classic in all credible forms of spirituality. From ancient times, spiritual seekers have sought isolated places in which to quiet themselves and come to a deeper recognition of who they are and to whom they belong. From the desert fathers and mothers trekking to the wilderness, to anchorites and anchoresses walling themselves into small cells, the desire to find spiritual balance through silence and solitude seems deeply ingrained in the human spirit.

I often hear about the longing for quiet from both individuals and groups. Silence as an endangered species is not just a perception by those beleaguered by the incessant racket of crowds, traffic, and ever-present technological devices. Gordon Hempton is an acoustic ecologist who tracks sounds in the Pacific Northwest. Silence, he notes, is not a lack of sound but a lack of noise. Without realizing it we are surrounded by the buzzing of appliances, computers, and other machines that hum away even while we are sleeping. Is it any wonder that so many of us are suffering from Nature Deficit Disorder and simply long for some peace and quiet? Psalm 42 describes this longing in exquisite fashion:

Why are you cast down, O my soul
and why are you disquieted within me?...
Deep calls to deep at the thunder of your cataracts;
all your waves and your billows have gone over me.
(*New Revised Standard Version Bible*)

The heaviness of the soul is coupled with a sense of "disquiet" in this lovely passage. When caught up in the activities of center ring, this longing may grow deeper and more acute. As an antidote to sound overload, the senses once again come into play.

Saint Teresa of Calcutta worked in some of the busiest—and noisiest—places in the world. This only heightened her awareness of Jesus' call to enter the inner room of the heart and to find the quieting needed to place herself in the center of divine love. By incorporating silence into our senses, she showed how we make our way toward a quieting of heart, mind, body, and soul. Saint Teresa's call to wed silence to the senses puts yet another spin on the FSSST prayer. Here is a paraphrase of her practice of inner silence:

Silence of the eyes—Look for the beauty and goodness of God, particularly in the small yet lovely details in the world around us. Soften your gaze in order to become more generous and forgiving when faced with the faults of others.

Silence of the ears—Strain to listen for the voice of God that can be heard in particular ways through the cries of those in need. Close the ears to gossip, slander, and violent speech.

Silence of the tongue—Speak the truth with love and use your voice to inspire hope, to restore dignity, and to promulgate joy and compassion. Measure your words carefully so that you refrain from saying anything that engenders fear, promotes violence, or causes pain to others and to yourself.

Silence of the mind—Open yourself to the truth and a deep understanding of God through meditative and contemplative prayer. Strive to rid the mind of all that dislodges it from the soul.

Silence of the heart—Seek to fulfill the Great Commandment by loving God wholeheartedly and embracing others, particularly those different from you, with mercy and compassion. Avoid anything that wounds or constricts the heart, such as selfishness, hatred, or greed.

Just as vital to reclaiming a place of silence in our lives is that of valuing solitude. No wonder these two practices go hand-in-hand. In an age when we can be connected to one another on a 24/7 basis, the longing to be offline and out of the mainstream runs deep. When Jesus withdrew for times of quiet and prayer, he sometimes brought a couple of his closest disciples with him. At other times, he wanted time by and for himself. It is a striking reminder of the need for solitude as a way to balance a very active ministry with a contemplative practice.

There is only so much time and energy we can give to performing in center ring. Withdrawing to the periphery refreshes, renews, and restores body, mind, heart, and soul. It also puts us back in touch with our truest, deepest selves. Otherwise, as Hildegard of Bingen says, we live in a "world that is not our own, in a world that is interpreted for us by others. An interpreted world is not a home. Part of the terror is to take back our own listening, to use our own voice, to see our own light." Often the time spent alone will, in turn, heighten our awareness of and appreciation for the companionship of others.

Are you intrigued or intimidated by silence and solitude? How does each practice play a part in your life?

DEVELOPING SOUL FRIENDSHIPS

The 1952 movie *The Greatest Show on Earth* begins with the solemn voice of director Cecil B. DeMille intoning the wonders of the circus. He calls it "a massive machine whose very life depends on discipline and motion and speed. A mechanized army on wheels…" The film tells the backstory of several performers, both in and out of the ring. If a tad melodramatic, the film shows the interdependence of the performers and that of the backstage crew. A tremendous bond holds the entire troupe together, each depending upon the skills and competence of the other.

Assuming the role of ringmaster can lead to the delusion that everything depends on us. This puts us in a lonely and isolated position. Wise ringmasters understand their role as facilitator, not overseer. In this way, they assist others in doing the best they can and open themselves to the help of others as well.

Celtic spirituality values the presence of "thin places"—geographical locations throughout Ireland and the British Isles where there is a thin divide between past, present, and future. These are places where one may encounter a more ancient reality—relationships beyond death that keep "soul friendships" alive. A key element of this spirituality is an appreciation of "little things" and the value of sharing them with others. The Celts had a great appreciation for relationships and the spiritualities of "soul friends." Saint Brigit, one of the most revered of the Celtic saints, is known for her ministry as a soul friend—a precursor to the spiritual director or companion.

Ron is my closest soul friend. We discovered long ago our mutual love of travel and our restless natures. I suppose a striking testimony to this is how we drove around the country together for an entire year and are still married! The Celtic value of "little things" also serves as a bond. When traveling, we don't try to see or do everything. Instead we pick a few places and spend a lot of time wandering around. On the surface we look like polar opposites. Ron is very athletic and runs road races up and down mountains. I love dance, music, and time with my books. The thread that binds us is a search for a life of meaning and an endless curiosity about what lies around the next bend in the road—both literally and metaphorically.

Even so, we could not have made it for as long as we have and in such smooth fashion without the encouragement, caring, and assistance of others. Family members and friends assured us of their love, support, and interest in what we were doing. My editors and coworkers at Sadlier helped me meet deadlines with flexibility and patience. The numerous hotel clerks, convenience store attendants, restaurant servers, housekeepers, park rangers, and other service providers were generous with their hospitality and helpfulness. Each relationship was part of a larger interconnected web that makes traveling through life not only possible but also grace-full. John of the Cross wrote, "God has so ordained things that we grow in faith only through the frail instrumentality of others." This web of interconnection reminds us of our own identity in relation to others and how it spreads outward to a much larger community and relationship with all of God's creatures.

Some of the greatest lessons to be learned about the "instrumentality of others" come not from other human beings but from animals. Boyd Varty grew up on the Londolozi Game Reserve in South Africa. As part of a TED talk, he described the way in which his understanding of the African concept of *"Ubuntu"* grew through watching the behavior of a herd of elephants. *Ubuntu* is often defined as the loving kindness we extend to each other, summed up in the phrase, "I am, because of you."

Varty describes a female elephant born with badly deformed hips and back legs. Her swiveling walk inspired the people at the game reserve to nickname her "Elvis." Varty didn't think the elephant would live long, but as they tracked with the herd over the next five years he saw her lumbering along with the rest of them. On one occasion he witnessed the elephants making their way down a slope to a watering hole. After having their fill, the matriarch turned and led the rest of the herd back up the slope. Elvis was last. With each attempt to climb the muddy hill her weak legs gave way and she slid back down. During the third attempt a young male moved behind her and used his trunk to provide the leverage needed for her to regain her footing. Varty went on to describe how the herd seemed to slow their progress in order to accommodate Elvis's slow movements. This touching realization caused him to rethink *Ubuntu* as "we are, because of all of us." It is not only a touching story but also a potent reminder of the value of kindness and of the interconnectedness of all life. Varty summed it up this way: "I believe that in the cathedral of the wild we get to see the most beautiful parts of ourselves reflected back at us" (*www.ted.com/talks/ boyd_varty_what_i_learned_from_nelson_mandela?language=en*).

What webs of connection have you created in your life? How do those reflect the concept of **Ubuntu**?

DISASSEMBLING THE TENT

The sukkot, like the big top, is temporary. Eventually, it is taken down, and life resumes its regular pace. Even so, something of the experience remains. Like pilgrims returning home from their journey, we are altered by the experience of pitching a tent. We are now ready to reenter center ring but with an expanded worldview and a transformed heart.

FOR REFLECTION AND DISCUSSION

Where are you able to pitch a tent in your life in order to find space for contemplation and reflection?

Who are those within and outside your tent that support, encourage, and inspire your spiritual growth?

CHAPTER FIVE

Reentering Center Ring

OUR ROAD TRIP ACROSS THE UNITED STATES WAS NOT THE FIRST TIME RON AND I EXITED CENTER RING IN SUCH A MAJOR WAY. Our first foray to the periphery took place over four decades ago when we each volunteered for the Frontier Apostolate. This missionary initiative was launched by Fergus O'Grady, bishop of the Diocese of Prince George, Canada, as a way to build and then staff Catholic schools across central British Columbia with volunteers from Canada, Ireland, the US, and the United Kingdom. Volunteers were given room and board and a stipend of $25 a month. They shared housing and meals together while each taking different roles in the school—as teachers and support staff.

I volunteered right out of college and recall my first terrifying night in Dawson Creek, a small town located on the eastern edge of the diocese and at the start of the Alcan Highway. "What have I done?" I kept asking myself. I didn't know a soul and was about to start my first teaching job far away from family and friends.. The following year I transferred to Fort St. James, an even more remote location. By then I was a seasoned volunteer, aware of the grace as well as the challenge of the mission. I recall the day I first saw Ron. He was standing on the back porch of the house where the women volunteers lived. His expression bore the same look of trepidation and uncertainty that I had known a year earlier. Like me he adjusted quickly, and together with the other volunteers we embarked on a year of tremendous challenge.

The school was populated by mostly First Nation children from the nearby reservation. Poverty, alcoholism, and domestic violence were rampant in their homes. After three years of turnover among the volunteers, the students had internalized a sense of rejection and decided in some unconscious fashion to meet the low expectations they assumed the staff had of them. Their behavior was out of control, making it difficult to maintain order in the classroom let alone teach. It took the better part of the year to gain their trust. Between the challenges at the school and our isolated location, we formed a strong bond as volunteers as well as with the pastor and the Irish Sisters of Mercy who also staffed the school. As is so often the case, the bigger the challenge, the richer the experience.

Our time in BC changed Ron and me profoundly and made for a difficult assimilation back into our lives in the US. "Ruined for life" is how the Jesuit Volunteer Corps was described by its founder, Father Jack Morris. It encapsulates the intensity of an experience that is both out of the mainstream and in the thick of life with those living on the margins. When Ron and I married a year later, we had come to terms with our shared desire for a life that was both centered and on the periphery, whatever that would come to mean.

TAKING FLIGHT

If I could run away and actually join the circus, I would be a trapeze artist. These performers swing back and forth with grace and then soar into midair with absolute trust that their partners will catch them. Trapeze artists even have their own song: "He flies through the air with the greatest of ease, that daring young man on the flying trapeze." The rhythm of the song matches the back-and-forth motion of the trapeze so that, in singing it, you're apt to bob your head from side to side. It's a song of abandon that encapsulates the joyous attitude of performers who leave anxiety behind and revel in those moments high above center ring.

Four months into our trip we stopped in Houston, where I had a speaking engagement at a national conference. While eating lunch with a group of colleagues, someone asked if we had a theme for our trip. Without giving it much thought, I quoted Thomas Merton: "This day will not come again." I had come across it a few weeks earlier while reading a compilation of his journals. Ron and I liked it so much we had it made into a bumper sticker, one that remains on our car to this day.

This isn't one of Merton's better-known quotes, and on the surface it doesn't sound very profound. He wrote it while seated on the front porch of his beloved hermitage, watching the beauty of a Kentucky sunrise. I found it on the same day we visited a beach in La Jolla, California. While Ron strolled up and down the sand snapping photos, I watched the waves cresting off the shoreline and pondered my early anxieties about the trip. It prompted a deeper understanding of Merton's thought. I realized with perfect clarity that I would likely never visit this exact spot again. That meant being present to where I was and what I was doing. At that same moment I spied a seal gliding across a breaking wave. Had I still been fragmented by anxiety I would have missed it. This simple experience reversed my first-night angst by changing the focus from what could go wrong. In a moment of sheer grace, the seal reminded me of all that was going right.

Staying in the moment—the classic definition of mindfulness—is one way of taking flight. The Buddhist monk Thich Nhat

Hanh describes this as keeping one's consciousness attuned to the present. Rather than fracturing time into separate pieces, we experience it in its fullness. He uses a mundane household task to illustrate what this means. "While washing the dishes one should only be washing the dishes, which means that while washing the dishes one should be completely aware of the fact that one is washing the dishes" (*The Miracle of Mindfulness*). Since washing dishes is far from my favorite task, being mindful of the moment takes some doing. It's not "flying through the air with the greatest of ease," but instead it grounds us in the present and opens up the possibility of finding joy in the simplest things.

When is it hard for you to maintain mindfulness,
to stay present to the moment?

TRAVELING SIMPLY

Every time I describe our trip to someone, I am inevitably asked one of two questions. The first is which state we liked the most. I always answer by saying each one had its unique aspects. It might sound like a dodge, but the truth is that there is no way to pick *a* best place on a trip that long and extensive. Much depended on the time of year. We were in Alabama in the spring, for example, when the dogwoods were in bloom and the water along the Gulf Coast was warm and pleasant. Had we visited New England in the dead of winter instead of the middle of a glorious autumn, our view of it would have been considerably altered. The reminder of how each day would not come again kept us alert and receptive. It felt like the description of Loki the dog having "the best day of its life for the 400th straight day." "I got to go outside! I got to sniff the bush!...I saw a squirrel and I barked at it and it ran up the tree! Then I came back inside, and the smoky-smelling tall man let me have a little piece of bacon…" (*The Onion*, October 13, 2004). A dog's simple pleasures—each marked with an exclamation point. This is how it felt as we experienced "best days" over and over again!

The other question was how we managed to travel for a whole year in such a small vehicle. Doing so took considerable calculation. I already described how we downsized, sold our house, and put most of our things in storage. Even so, our first attempt at packing the car was a disaster. Suitcases jutted over our heads and bundles of supplies poked out from between the seats. That was not only a hazard but also uncomfortable. We unpacked everything and started over. This meant reassessing our basic needs and how we might live with less. We took off with a full load but also with room to see out the rear window and enough space in which to relax. In mid-summer we made our way back to Colorado for a two-week break and a visit with family and friends. While staying with my brother, we unpacked the entire car and marveled at the unnecessary things we were carrying. What first seemed essential was now superfluous. When we took off for the second half of our trip it was with a much lighter load.

One of the biggest obstacles to exiting center ring is the stuff that clutters our lives. Material accumulations are only the tip of the iceberg; what lies beneath is much harder to jettison. Consider the mental and emotional detritus that becomes a drag on our minds and hearts. Unattended schemas and ongoing battles with the past. Smoldering resentments and toxic relationships. Anger, fear, anxiety, and dread. The list goes on and on. Finding spiritual balance requires letting go, an ongoing process that takes time, intention, and a great deal of inner work. If we aren't willing to do this, we reenter center ring with the same burdens with which we exited it.

Just as we exit center ring with a Sabbath mindset, we reenter in the same way. Wayne Mueller describes "thinning" as an important aspect of Sabbath keeping. This makes space for life. Gardens, he notes, only grow when thinned out. The same holds true for the spiritual life. If we don't make space, our souls eventually choke to death from lack of nourishment and an overgrowth of toxic elements. Spiritual thinning empties out the false self—the performer that masks who we truly are.

We live in a culture that trains us to be in control—of our thoughts and emotions, our finances and future, our possessions and power. Spiritual energy, however, cannot be managed and manipulated. In order to open to it we must let go and become smaller. This is called *kenosis*—a word taken from the Greek *keno*, which means "to empty." Such self-emptying makes room for God to enter the spaces previously occupied by our own egos and self-will. Paul, in his letter to the Philippians, describes the kenosis that Jesus underwent. "He emptied himself, taking the form of a slave, coming in human likeness; and found human in appearance, he humbled himself, becoming obedient to death, even death on a cross" (Philippians 2:7–8).

This humbling process is sometimes erroneously equated with self-abasement and shame. As Thomas Merton wryly observed, "Humility is a virtue, not a neurosis." Shadow work entails an honest look at our false selves and looking beyond them to what the Zen masters describe as "the face you had before you were born." Richard Rohr, the Franciscan teacher and author, writes, "This metaphysical self cannot die and always lives in God; it is your True Self, and is probably what we mean by the soul" ("Embracing the Shadow," Richard Rohr's Daily Reflection, Friday July 15, 2016). The beauty of this work is the way in which it opens us to the mysterious working of God in both the light and dark spaces of life. The task of shadow work isn't to eliminate either but to integrate them. As Rohr points out, we cannot see when immersed in total light or total darkness. We only find our sight when there is enough light to illuminate the darkness and enough darkness to mitigate the glare of the light.

How have you come to recognize and embrace the shadow part of yourself?

GOD IN THE SHADOWS

As we moved further along the road, I continued to ponder the images of God I would be describing on the retreat for the Episcopal women's group when we returned to Colorado. At the same time, Ron's photography began to include more and more shots of reflections—abstract images that were intriguing and somewhat mysterious. We were also making a lot of visits to battlegrounds, cemeteries, and national memorials. These were both haunting and hopeful. Places like Gettysburg or the 9/11 crash site in Shanksville, Pennsylvania, brought to mind the horrific toll of war and terrorism. These experiences, along with Kay's dollars, continued to remind us of the shadows of human heartache. They served as a reminder that we need not flee from the shadow moments in our lives.

God as Mystery began to emerge in these experiences. It is an image that is paradoxically immanent and transcendent. "God," as Marcus Borg has said, "is the name we use for the nonmaterial stupendous, wondrous 'More' that includes the universe even as God transcends the universe. This is God as the 'encompassing Spirit,' the one in whom 'we live and move and have our being,' the one who is all around us and within us. God is the one in whom the universe is, even as God is more than the universe; the Mystery who is beyond all names, even as we name the sacred Mystery in our various ways" (*The Heart of Christianity*). This might be the most evocative image of all, one that jars us out of our assumptions and self-righteousness and into a wider worldview. After time on the periphery we return to center ring with a deepened awareness of and empathy for those whose lives are filled with shadows, and with an assurance that our own shadows will not overtake us.

THE KENOSIS OF FORGIVENESS

Most of our energy is emotional. This is why we can wake up in the morning after a good night's sleep feeling ready to plunge into our day with enthusiasm. Run into a traffic jam on the highway, encounter an uncooperative coworker, or have a fight with your teenage child, and all that good energy dissipates in a heartbeat. We reach the end of the day feeling dragged out even though we did nothing physically taxing. Loss of emotional energy is one of the greatest factors in feeling off-kilter. And nothing drains emotional energy like resentment, anger, and guilt. An antidote to each is forgiveness.

Forgiveness is one of the most vital forms of kenosis—an emptying out of the toxins of resentment toward others as well as our own inner shame or neurotic guilt. Henri Nouwen described forgiveness as "the name of love practiced among people who love poorly." When we 'fess up by acknowledging how and when we have loved poorly we begin to recognize the redemptive power of forgiveness.

Forgiveness was, of course, central to Jesus' teaching. It's mentioned twice in the Our Father—"forgive us our trespasses as we forgive those who trespass against us." This makes forgiveness a two-way street—one in which we both seek and extend the forgiveness that will empty our hearts of anything that prevents us from loving well.

The original meaning of the word "sin" is to "miss the mark." Sin throws us off center, and we fall short in our efforts to love God, others, and ourselves. Think what it means to "trespass" on others—to violate their space, to trample on their feelings, to ignore the boundaries of a respectful and loving relationship. In seeking forgiveness from those wounded by our off-the-mark words and behavior, we face up to what we did or failed to do (conversion), we acknowledge the harm done (confession), and we embrace the peace that comes with letting go of all that binds us to a small and wounded self (celebration). This requires an honest look at ourselves—a humbling process that brings us face-to-face with our flaws as well as our strengths. Great mystics and spiritual writers understood how such knowledge strips away the facade and reveals who we are at the deepest level. It's not easy work, but it is necessary if we are to grow more fully alive.

THE POWER OF FORGIVING

The last national monument we visited on our trip was the Oklahoma City Memorial—site of the 1995 act of domestic terrorism. After having been to several battlegrounds and cemeteries, I didn't expect to be so moved by the memorial. The street where the truck containing the explosives once stood is now a beautiful reflecting pool. Chairs representing each of the victims killed in the attack are placed on the lawn above it. Most touching of all are the smaller chairs memorializing the little children killed in the daycare center inside the Alfred P. Murrah Federal Building. It wasn't until I viewed Ron's photos later in the evening that I saw the teddy bear placed on one of these—a sweet and touching symbol of grief over those so innocent and undeserving of such a horrific death.

That I could find such peace in a place devastated by carnage and terror was remarkable. Even so, this is what I found in other sites, such as Gettysburg, Arlington, and Shanksville. It's another example of the paradox of the paschal mystery: beauty arising from the ashes, peace replacing violence, "swords beaten into plowshares." While all of those affected by the brutal realities of bombings and battles may not be able to yet forgive, there is hope arising from what may be possible when we grieve the losses we suffer and seek healing. Forgiveness makes both possible.

The root of the word forgive is "to let go, to give back, to cease to harbor." When we let go, we discover a way to find rest and respite from our judgments and resentments. Without forgiveness, we become tethered to the one who has harmed us or to the painful experiences of the past. In forgiving, we take back control of our fates and our feelings. Doing so also helps us extend the forgiveness others ask of us. This makes forgiveness an empowering process, one in which we cease to cling to bitterness and to give others power over us. A healed memory is not necessarily a deleted one, however. Instead we are provided a new form of memory by changing past hurts into a hopeful future. "To forgive," says Wayne Mueller, "is to bear what we are given...to acknowledge that we have been afflicted with pain, loss, or harm, but to bless it all and let it be—to take refuge in God" (*Learning to Pray*). This makes us larger than the sum of all trespasses against us.

When or how have you experienced
the power of forgiveness?

FORGIVING OURSELVES

Several years ago I was asked to offer a talk on time management to a group of publishing consultants. The planners of the conference engaged the talents of a small circus troupe to tie together the themes of each presentation. Speakers were given a topic related to a particular circus skill and then put in touch with the corresponding performer. I was assigned the juggler—a perfect fit for the topic of managing time. In the course of the pre-work for the talk, I had an opportunity to interview him about the various items he juggled as well as how he did it. His answers enlightened me further about the scope of his talent. One response stood out among all the others. "What one essential thing do you need to be a juggler?" I asked him. "Is it coordination? Flexibility? Dexterity?" To each of these he responded no and explained that, with time and practice, one could develop these skills. Then he shared the secret to becoming a juggler. "The most important thing is the ability to forgive your-self." He went on to explain how forgiveness was a necessity when dropping the balls: "Otherwise you will never pick them up and try again."

When considering who needs forgiving in our lives, we often bypass ourselves. Perhaps this is why so many people reach adulthood with chronic shame-and-blame patterns that are so difficult to break. The schemas we develop can perplex and overwhelm us. Is this the struggle Paul described in doing the very thing he hated? The desert fathers understood Paul's dilemma. They described the "passions" that inhibited them from being their truest selves and alienated them from God's infinite mercy. Unlike the manner in which we describe passion today, their definition had to do with any state of mind, desire, or behavior that was destructive to themselves or to others.

Three intertwining passions seem to predominate in our time:

Perfectionism: the secret belief that our true identity comes from what we do and how we do it rather than from God. Variations of this passion include overdoing, underdoing (procrastination out of fear of failure), and non-doing (the inability to make changes out of fear of the unknown). This can apply to any of the circus performers we become when unrealistic expectations are placed upon us.

Judgmentalism: placing a distortion of perfectionism on other people. Just as we have expectations placed upon us by others, we turn around and do the same to them. This shows itself in continuous criticism of and complaining about those who irritate, annoy, or disagree with us. We might observe how this works by paying attention to what obsesses us. It often says more about us than another person.

Despair: The conviction that we have committed sins so grievous we must give up our right to make claims on the people around us. Despair is the ultimate passion because it gives up on the self altogether. We quit the circus performer of our dreams out of a descent into hopelessness. The next step is giving up on God.

To be agents and recipients of forgiveness, we need to recognize our own belovedness. This identity does not come from the performances we perfect to meet external or internal expectations; it comes from God. This is the True Self that can never be given away or stolen. No wonder that, when Jesus extended forgiveness to others, it was often to those most adept at seeing with an inner eye. Their *faith* saved them—not from external forces but from a chronic sense of unworthiness, false pride, and despair. So often it was holding to a slender thread of humility and poverty of spirit. This made them receptive to the deepest kind of healing and opened their hearts to the good news of God's immense mercy. Paul's letter to the Ephesians is a forceful reminder of the importance of forgiveness and mercy for both individuals and communities. "All bitterness, fury, anger, shouting, and reviling must be removed from you, along with all malice. [And] be kind to one another, compassionate, forgiving one another as God has forgiven you in Christ" (Ephesians 4:31–32). If anything is going to offer spiritual balance, it is the call to mercy and compassion and away from anything that blocks it. We must make intentional choices about what to carry back into center ring.

FINDING MY CENTER

Toward the end of our trip, I came to a realization of the center rings I no longer wanted or needed to reenter. The expanse of time and space afforded a view of the center ring from the edges. I could more easily identify which activities weren't bringing me life, such as the committee work mentioned in Chapter 2. I also had enough distance to recognize the relationships that were draining me of emotional energy and the decisions I might make about the road ahead of me. Our trip had indeed become a sabbatical.

It doesn't matter if the move to the periphery happens over the course of a year or a day. I have had similar realizations while on a weekend retreat or even during the course of a long walk. The length of the journey matters little; what does matter is the intentional move away from the center of perpetual motion. Each Sabbath experience brings us closer to the center ring that matters most—our truest selves.

I have to confess that the language of the true self/false self eluded me for quite a while. Learning more about the "two halves of life," a phrase popularized by Carl Jung, brought it into better focus. In his daily blog Richard Rohr summarized these as follows: "The first half of life is spent building our sense of identity, importance, and security—what I would call the false self and Freud might call the ego self...In the second half of life, the ego still has a place, but now in the service of the True Self or soul, your inner and inherent identity" (Richard Rohr's Daily Meditation, October 12, 2015).

The first half of life is about *acquiring* possessions, titles, success, structure, and an external "container" in which to place everything. This isn't a bad thing; quite the contrary. There is a need for this in order to acquire a sense of identity and what Jung called a healthy ego structure. It is also, however, where we begin to take on those circus performances that throw us off-kilter. Inevitably the balls come crashing down or the tightrope frays as our ego structures fail to hold up. For those undergoing transformation through the process of the broken-open heart, the container becomes inconsequential and matters much less than the contents. Jung described it as forging an ego that can stand on its own, "an ego that endures, that endures the truth, and that is capable of coping with the world and with fate. Then, to experience defeat is also to experience victory."

This has less to do with age than experience. I know young adults who have crossed the tragic gap and come out the other side with wisdom and grace. On the other hand, there are older people who haven't done a bit of self-reflection and continue to operate under the illusion that their possessions and prestige reflect their true worth.

The tightrope walker understands the risk of falling. As she makes her way across the high wire she must constantly stop and restore her balance. "We must dare to lose our balance, and yet keep it," David Steindl-Rast says. "We must dare to make fools of ourselves but be careful not to do it foolishly. Faith is the art of making fools of ourselves wisely like dancers" (*Gratefulness, the Heart of Prayer*). Failure, disappointment, grief, and loss are often the experiences that bridge the two halves of life. Rather than fearing, denying, suppressing, or wallowing in them, we learn to walk through them and find our way home once again. Finding spiritual balance is not a matter of perfection but of purpose. The humility that comes with kenosis brings this kind of balance.

How are you experiencing/have you experienced the "two halves of life"?

MOVING INTO WHOLENESS

It would be wonderful to think that the second half of life will place us in perfect balance but, unfortunately, that is not the case. If anything, we become more attuned to the ways we are off-balance. The good news is, now that it has risen into our consciousness, we can make decisions that will move us toward wholeness.

Let's revisit the account of Martha and Mary. In her book *Centering Prayer and Inner Awakening*, Cynthia Bourgeault describes Martha as the embodiment of *ordinary awareness*. She goes about her tasks with efficiency and a sense of purpose. In the Lucan account, she is also stressed and whiny. This typifies ordinary awareness. We think our performances are worthy of center ring, and we want others to notice us and applaud our efforts. Mary, on the other hand, embodies *spiritual awareness*. She sits at the feet of Jesus, mesmerized by his teaching and absorbed in the present moment. It doesn't matter whether anyone else approves of her.

Rather than pitting these two against one another—one being "right" and the other "wrong"—Bourgeault notes how each state of awareness is necessary for functioning in this world. "The idea in spiritual transformation is to integrate and reprioritize these levels so that our ordinary awareness is in alignment with and in service to our spiritual awareness (which in turn…is in service to divine awareness). In that alignment our being flows rightly, from innermost out." This enables us to meet our responsibilities and carry out daily tasks with enough inner strength to do so. The grounding we have in spiritual awareness flows out of "divine abundance" without any egoist needs for attention, affirmation, or recognition.

There is a Martha and a Mary in each one of us. Moving out of center ring for Sabbath time gives rise to a strengthening of Mary-like attentiveness and reverence. "There are incredible luminous depths within," says Bourgeault, "in which we know how to listen and to whom we are listening." Once we learn how and where to find these, we come home to ourselves once again. We are also less likely to be thrown off balance when our ordinary awareness is overshadowed by grief, loss, and failure.

In *The Interior Castle*, Teresa of Ávila describes the kind of inward journey that brings us home to ourselves. In the introduction to her translation of this beautiful work, Mirabai Starr writes: "From the center of the soul, Teresa teaches, God is calling. The driving force of our existence is our longing to find our way home to [God]. This quest involves passage through the seven essential chambers of the interior castle. The doorway to the castle is contemplative prayer." The immersion into each dwelling provides a deep way to be in union with God. It's not without its setbacks, however, something Teresa readily acknowledges. Thus we need ways to draw back to ourselves in order to open our hearts to God's loving presence. One of the ways to do this is through the Prayer of Recollection in which the soul remembers and rebuilds the place where it can go to pray and retakes control from the distractions that can assail the senses. This is a critical form of prayer when we are thrown off-kilter by setbacks and rude awakenings, by too much responsibility and too little rest, by the wild beasts that seem beyond taming. In recollecting ourselves, we recall those places where we can pitch a tent and retreat into it for some much-needed Sabbath time. In doing so, we find ourselves once again.

TURNING TOWARD HOME

Oklahoma was the final state on our itinerary. It took us 40,000 miles to reach a state we could have visited on the first day. Despite our eagerness to be back in Colorado and to establish a home once again, we took time to visit two wildly different places—the Oklahoma City Memorial and Cadillac Ranch (where a dozen 1950s Cadillac are planted, tails-up, in a remote cow pasture). It was satisfying to know that we were still engaged enough with the trip to step out once more.

We spent the last night of our trip in Santa Fe, New Mexico, bringing us full circle and ready to reenter the center ring of home. This meant more than finding another house to live in, however.

While strolling around Santa Fe once more I slipped into a bookstore and came across the book by Ann Armbrecht that I mentioned in Chapter 2. Much like us, her departure after a lengthy time of research in Nepal left her questioning the whole concept of home. It was not a specific structure or geographical place. "It meant opening to the reality of my life, stripped away of any story to justify what I had done, and seeing that I was responsible for the world in which I lived, the sweetness and the poison, as much as by my action as my inaction." The only way to face such a reality is by coming home to ourselves and discovering anew that inner space of balance. Thomas Merton put it another way: *"Our real journey in life is interior: it is a matter of growth, deepening, and of an ever greater surrender to the creative action of love and grace in our hearts."*

Before we left on our trip, both Ron and I expressed the hope that something in our lives would somehow shift by the time we reached its end. I am not sure that we expected that change to be more internal than external but so it was. We had ideas about what we each wanted to do once we had a permanent address—to find a house on the periphery and to write a book about our experiences. We did both. The book, *The Long Road to Oklahoma*, took two years to write—twice as long as the trip itself. We found the house on the final day of the trip as we drove from Santa Fe to Denver. My niece Tracy is a realtor, and she emailed some listings to consider. One was a townhouse located less than five miles from the stop we made on the first day of the trip. Ron saw a train approaching and pulled onto the turnoff toward the town of Larkspur, Colorado, to shoot some pictures. It seemed more than a little significant that we were so close to our eventual home.

It has taken longer for the internal changes to surface, and I suppose those are still in the works. When I began working on the theme of spiritual balance—something I first offered as a one-hour presentation and eventually as a weekend retreat, our road trip kept working its way into it. Lessons like stepping out, traveling lightly, pitching a tent, and "this day will not come again" began to surface and deepen as I continued to ponder the key to a balanced spiritual life. When all is said and done, it has to do with integration and wholeness.

LOVE AT THE CENTER

When we were in St. Louis, Ron took a picture of the Gateway Arch while he was standing directly underneath it. The arch cuts across the center of the photo, narrowing in the middle and fanning out on either end. It resembles a different kind of tightrope—one that is not straight and narrow but curved and uneven. Even so, there is symmetry to the tightrope, one that strikes a balance between its two outer edges.

In the first chapter I described how we can be thrown off-kilter by the various expectations placed upon us by others and ourselves. Doing so can result in becoming the performer we think we should be rather than the one we truly are. In truth, we may well be proficient at multiple circus acts. If we, in fact, step into various roles in whole-hearted fashion, we will find ourselves capable of some pretty amazing feats. Instead of being thrown off-kilter we are able to strike a balance between the active and the contemplative, the Martha and the Mary, the center ring and the periphery. The secret is to complete each act with love.

In his book *Common Sense Spirituality*, David Steindl-Rast describes the return to our inmost heart as a mystical point of contact with the transcendent: "There, at the very core of our being, we encounter the nearness of that Mystery, which surrounds all things beyond the farthest horizon. In discovering this polarity of center and periphery, we discover our own life as the Cosmic Tree springing up from the taproot of creation and branching out into a region beyond space and time. We discover Mystery at the center of our own heart and sense the staggering possibility that our little life may become ultimately meaningful as celebration of that Mystery in which it is rooted."

The center ring in which we will find spiritual balance is not found in the entrenched circus acts we create or in the drifter's life on the road. The center is within. It's our own hearts, the true "dwelling places" Jesus described to his disciples in his farewell discourse (see John 14:2). Rather than waiting to discover them in a life after this, we are invited to move toward them here and now.

Reentering center ring with a deepened sense of spiritual awareness is all about love. "When I find my heart," says Steindl-Rast, "I also find the courage to be myself, for the heart stands for the very self." Our pursuits and distractions, our fears and anxieties, our false selves and outsized expectations—all are brought into balance by love. With it we are able to walk tightropes strung between engagement and withdrawal. To face the wild beasts of schemas run amuck and to face the shadow sides of ourselves. To bear the weight of sorrow, particularly with those pushed to the periphery by suffering and need. To take flight through a mindful awareness of the moment and to find joy in all of God's creation. To laugh with delight and revel in everything that comes our way each day. To join the great circus of life in all of its glorious diversity and to draw others into its circle of forgiveness, compassion, and mercy. If love is at the center of who we are and what we do, of our ordinary awareness and our spiritual awareness, then we will find the balance that allows us to respond to every off-kilter moment with grace, gratitude, and a spirit of adventure.

FOR REFLECTION AND DISCUSSION

When do you find yourself most open to discover
love at the center of your life?

What center rings do you want to reenter?
Which ones do you no longer need or want?

How are you able to find spiritual balance
in an off-kilter world?

A POEM, A PRAYER,
AND PARTING THOUGHTS

A POEM

I first came across Lynn Ungar's beautiful poem in Wayne Mueller's book *Sabbath*. It is an evocative image of the field to which Jesus calls us—away from our anxieties and center-ring concerns to the periphery of trust and enjoyment. I am most grateful to Ms. Ungar for her generous permission to reprint the poem, as it makes such a fitting link with the life of spiritual balance.

Camas Lilies

Consider the lilies of the field,
the blue banks of camas opening
into acres of sky along the road.
Would the longing to lie down
and be washed by that beauty
abate if you knew their usefulness,
how the natives ground their bulbs
for flour, how the settlers' hogs
uprooted them, grunting in gleeful
oblivion as the flowers fell?

And you—what of your rushed and
useful life? Imagine setting it all down—
papers, plans, appointments, everything—
leaving only a note: "Gone

to the fields to be lovely. Be back
when I'm through with blooming,"

Even now, unneeded and uneaten,
the camas lilies gaze out above the grass
from their tender blue eyes.
Even in sleep your life will shine.
Make no mistake. Of course
your work will always matter.
Yet Solomon in all his glory
was not arrayed like one of these.

A PRAYER

One of my favorite collections of prayers is Ted Loder's *Guerrillas of Grace*. His poetic voice is both inspirational and down-to-earth. I can't think of a more fitting way to end this book on spiritual balance—with its metaphors of the circus and cross-country travel—than by including Loder's prayer for "an enchantment of the heart." I am grateful to Augsburg Books for their gracious permission to reprint the prayer in this book.

"Grant Me an Enchantment of Heart"
by **TED LODER**

O God of children and clowns, as well as martyrs and bishops,
somehow you always seem to tumble a jester or two of light
through the cracks of my proud defense
into the shadows of my sober piety.

Grant me, now, an enchantment of heart that,
for a moment,
the calliope of your kingdom
may entice my spirit, laughing,
out of my sulky pre-occupations
into a childlike delight
in the sounds and silence that hum of grace;

so I may learn again that life is never quite as serious as I suppose,
yet more precious than I dare take for granted,
even for a moment;

that I may be released into the possibilities of the immediate,
and rush, smudge souled as I am,
to join the parade of undammed fools
who see the ridiculous in the sublime,
the sublime in the ridiculous;
and so dare to take pratfalls for love,
walk tightropes for justice,
tame lions for peace,
and rejoice to travel light,
knowing there is little I have or need
except my brothers and sisters to love,
you to trust
and your stars to follow home.

PARTING THOUGHTS

Spend time with Lynn Ungar's poem and consider the note you might leave behind as you exit center ring. Savor Ted Loder's prayer and its imagery of clowns and calliopes, of walking tightropes and taming lions, of being soul smudged and a proud participant in the parade of fools seeking a glimpse of the Divine in the world around us and in the stars above. May your own search for spiritual balance bring an enchantment of the heart that transform the off-kilter moments into ones of grace.

Travel well and with an open heart.

Kathy Hendricks

APPENDIX
From Performance to Practice

Performances are meant for others to observe and admire. They are essentially made for the ego. To engage in practice, however, is to move deeper into the soul. This not only draws us into the center of ourselves but also serves those around us. In the preceding chapters I mentioned several spiritual practices that help to achieve the latter. Here is a more extensive look at what they entail. Choose ones that affirm your own quest for spiritual balance as well as ones that might stretch you a bit farther.

BREATHING PRAYERS

The most simple, basic, and universal form of prayer is simply breathing. From ancient times, the breath has been used as a way to calm the mind and center the heart. Thich Nhat Hanh describes the breath as that which connects life to consciousness. "Whenever your mind becomes scattered, use your breath as the means to take hold of [it] again" (*Miracle of Mindfulness*). The process is straightforward: take in a deep breath and then breathe it out in a conscious act of exhalation. Concentrate all effort on this simple two-step practice. With each breath it often becomes easier to take in more air and to let it out in slower fashion. When thoughts and distractions crop up, clear them out again by pulling the mind back to breathing in and breathing out. The calming effect of this simple practice is almost instantaneous. Another way to practice this prayer is by using a short phrase or word that helps to re-focus attention and let go of stray thoughts. My personal favorite is the psalm verse "Be still and know that I am God" (Psalm 46:11).

I also use breathing as a way to pray traditional prayers, such as the Our Father. Breathing in one line ("Our Father") and breathing out the next ("who art in heaven") has a calming effect when I feel distracted or anxious. I also find myself meditating more deeply on the words as I take them into my heart.

CENTERING PRAYER

This form of contemplative prayer is "a receptive method of silent prayer that prepares us to receive the gift of contemplative prayer, prayer in which we experience God's presence within us, closer than breathing, closer than thinking, closer than consciousness itself. [It] is both a relationship with God and a discipline to foster that relationship." (Source: Contemplative Outreach—contemplativeoutreach.org)

A resurgence of interest in this form of prayer can be attributed, in large part, to the work of Father Thomas Keating, a Trappist monk who sought to reintroduce the ancient practice of Christian meditation at a time when many young people were turning to Eastern spiritual practices. It involves an emptying of thoughts through sustained periods of silence. The use of a single, one-syllable word, such as "God" or "peace," draws the soul back to itself when it is drawn away by distractions. There are many good books on this prayer practice, and the website listed above is a helpful place to access more information about it.

THE EXAMEN

The Examen is part of a regular regimen that recognizes God's presence in the midst of daily events and experiences and discerns God's direction for our lives. It forms part of a larger spiritual practice called the Spiritual Exercises as developed by Saint Ignatius Loyola, founder of the Society of Jesus (Jesuits). It is a practice most often used at the end of the day and entails five steps:

Place yourself in God's presence. One of the reasons we tend to be reactive rather than responsive is that we don't take time to reflect. This first step invites us to go back over our day and to recall those events, experiences, and people that were part of it. This is something like the keeping of a mental log—a way to recollect where we have been, what we have done, and who we have been with.

Pray for the grace to understand how God is acting in your life. Negative experiences tend to stick in our minds more easily than positive ones so this next step in the Examen is quite significant. Gratitude often arises by recalling the small things—those people or experiences that might be overlooked without some dedicated reflection.

Review your day—recall specific moments and your feelings at the time. When we stifle our emotions, particularly those that are uncomfortable, embarrassing, or even shameful, we deny a certain part of who we are. This step in the Examen can provide another way across the tragic gap described in Chapter 3 by moving from reaction to response. The regular practice of reviewing each day builds the capacity to sort out reactive ways of being and then to develop responsive ones.

Reflect on what you did, said, or thought in these instances. This part of the Examen invites us more fully into kenosis—an emptying of our self-preoccupation in order to allow God's Spirit to fill us. We ask God for direction toward something in our day that needs attention. This might be a feeling, a behavior, or an encounter. Once again, we may discover that the most significant parts of our days aren't the big things but those that we might otherwise bypass. We give ourselves over to prayer, allowing it to rise in us. This might lead to asking for forgiveness, seeking guidance, or giving thanks.

Look toward tomorrow and how you might collaborate more completely with God's plan. This is a particularly hopeful part of the Examen process. Even if we reach the end of a day feeling exhausted, drained, or discouraged, we look ahead to what the next day might bring. It's important to be specific so that we don't just make vague resolutions but intentionally move toward open-heartedness. The Examen ends with the Our Father, a prayer that could be breathed, as noted above, in order to keep it from becoming a rote recitation.

INTERCESSION

To intercede means to "ask on behalf of." We turn our attention outward, toward the needs of others. In Chapter 3 I told the story of Kay's dollars and how they opened me up to those pushed to the periphery by grief, loss, failure, or desperation. This, in turn, inspired prayers of intercession. Such prayer is a profound way to expand our spiritual horizons beyond our own particular concerns and to remind us of our common bond as human beings. When we pray on behalf of others, we increase our capacity for compassion. When others pray for us, we are reminded that we are not meant to go it alone.

Of all the accounts in the New Testament, the Prayer of Jesus in John 17 touches my heart the most. The entire passage is so intimate, showing concern, love, and deep affection for the group of disciples who have become Jesus' closest friends as well as for all those "who will believe in me through their word" (vs. 20). While I often turn to this text for comfort, I also try to pay attention to its more challenging aspects. Jesus doesn't pray, for example, that his disciples be spared discomfort, disappointment, or even pain. He recognizes what lies ahead for them and asks for what they truly need. This was a hallmark of Jesus' prayer for others, not just in his final hours but throughout his ministry. He didn't pray for a quick fix but for faith over the long haul

I once read that intercessory prayer shouldn't seek to patch others up. Instead we must pray them into the life of God. It has taken me a long time to recognize how my prayers of intercession for people I love are often for their circumstances rather than for them. The latter is a much more difficult way to pray. So much easier to ask for a miracle cure, a financial windfall, or a simple solution to a complex problem. Praying, as Jesus did, for another's well-being, for their joy, and for life in God, takes strength and trust. This doesn't mean ignoring the circumstances that create heartache and distress but truly giving them over to God whose depth of mercy and understanding is far greater than we can imagine.

JOURNALING

I have kept a journal since I was eleven years old. Granted, those early entries were more of a log of daily activities and, later, a litany of adolescent angst. At some level, however, the writing was expressive of my feelings and became my own form of the Examen without my realizing it. At a point in my twenties, the journal took an intentional turn towards the spiritual. I began ending each entry with a prayer—a practice that has held to this day.

I know some people who would rather scrub toilets than write in a journal. I suppose part of this comes from a dread of writing long entries or trying to express one's thoughts on paper. While my daily journals run to full notebook pages, there are other ways to utilize this spiritual practice. In Chapter 4 I described my experience of keeping a gratitude journal. It consisted of one or two lines at the most and yet opened up many insights and provided relief during a time of great stress.

Various studies have been done on the psychological benefits of writing out one's thoughts and feelings. In an online blog, Gregory Ciotti lists some of these. "Expressive writing has also been linked to improved mood, well-being, and reduced stress levels for those who do it regularly… Moreover, laziness with words creates difficulty in describing feelings, sharing experiences, and communicating with others" ("The Psychological Benefits of Writing Regularly," July 15, 2016, Lifehacker.com). These benefits underscore the value of writing for spiritual balance. It offers one more way to counter the off-kilter moments through periods of reflection as well as an opening into deeper self-knowledge.

LECTIO DIVINA

Lectio divina (sacred reading) is a spiritual practice that opens up the texts of Scripture (along with other forms of spiritual reading) and looks deeper into them through meditation, prayer, and contemplation. It moves us from the head, where we can get stuck in cerebral pursuits, to the heart, where the word of God rests most comfortably. *Lectio divina* first appears in writing in the Rule of Benedict and constitutes not only a form of prayer but also a way of life in Benedictine spirituality. Benedict's invitation to "listen with the ear of your heart" draws us into a spaciousness with God's word, one that deepens as we move into the process.

There are four movements in *lectio divina*. It revolves around a single passage from Scripture, read four times, and then moves us deeper into reflection and insight into the text with each step.

Lectio/Listen—This first movement is a simple listening to the text. It's preferable to read the passage aloud so the words can move beyond the mind and reverberate in the heart. Author James Finley notes lectio's potential to deliver us from the temptation to think or to say something too soon. He calls it "sustained receptivity to a beauty not yet thought about."

Meditatio/meditate—Meditating upon the text draws us further into it through establishing a connection with it. This doesn't mean we pull out the concordance and delve into exegesis. By remaining centered in the heart, we open ourselves to flashes or tastes of insight. This, in turn, cultivates inner understanding.

Oratio/pray—We move into praying the text, sometimes in wordless form. We let arise in us that which inspires us, draws us closer to God, and weans us away from self-reliance so that we can give ourselves over totally to God's will and desire.

Contemplatio/contemplate—We then step back and give the word space, allowing it to rest in us as we rest in God. Words become unnecessary as the text finds a place within our emptied-out heart.

As a way of life, *lectio divina* can be drawn into one's entire day. We might begin with the sacred reading and listening in the morning, meditate upon its meaning as we move into the day's activities, allow prayer to arise in us as the day unfolds, and rest with it as we approach the day's end.

MEDITATION

The practice of meditation entails periods of silence in which we make a concerted effort to seek a greater understanding of God and of our faith. I've already noted how meditation fits into the process of breathing prayer, *lectio divina*, and other practices that entail emptying the mind of thoughts and distractions.

There have been various ways to practice meditation, from the perspective of Eastern spiritual traditions and those of the West. One of the most ancient is through the use of prayer beads. The act of meditating with a circle of beads worn on the wrist or passing through the fingers is a calming experience that is partnered with reflection. The Catholic Rosary reflects on the life, death, resurrection, and ascension of Jesus Christ through the repetition of familiar prayers that focus the mind and heart on these great mysteries of faith. Buddhist prayer beads or "malas" count the number of times a mantra is recited, breaths are taken in, prostrations are made, or the Buddha's name is said. In both cases, the repetitive nature of the practice serves to empty the mind and draw one toward a deeper level of awareness.

PRAYER WALKING

Prayer walking is an intentional spiritual practice that dates back many centuries. Monasteries, abbeys, and cathedrals were often constructed with a cloister—a covered walk or open gallery that ran alongside the walls of the building. It was a concrete way of separating those living a monastic life from the rest of the world. Cloisters formed a natural path in which one might walk in unimpeded fashion so as to enter into contemplation or study.

There are various forms of prayer walking. One is a pilgrimage—a journey taken to a holy place in order to become closer to God. Some people take pilgrimages to the Holy Land or to a special church, shrine, temple, or mosque, for holy days or times of prayer. Over time, people of all faiths have embarked on such journeys as a way to deepen their faith. The key to making a good pilgrimage is being open to how it might change and strengthen us by the time we get home.

During the course of our yearlong trip, we took shorter pilgrimages to places we each regarded as sacred. One of these, for me, was the tomb of Abraham Lincoln in Springfield, Illinois. I have long been an admirer of Lincoln and his great store of wisdom and insight. Standing at the site of his grave was a profoundly moving experience.

We also found other places made sacred by the meaning of the sacrifices offered (such as the cemeteries at Arlington and Gettysburg) or the lives taken (such as Oklahoma City, Shanksville, and Ground Zero). Visits to these places could never be made in short order; instead we spent hours walking quietly among the graves or pondering the memorial plaques and structures. Then there were the sites that slowed us down simply because of the magnificence that surrounded us—a gorgeous rose garden in Portland,

Oregon, or Sequoia National Park, for example. Each one drew us into the kind of reverence that gave way to praise, thanksgiving, and blessing.

Another form of prayer walking is that of the labyrinth. Unlike a maze, which has no central destination, the labyrinth follows several routes, or circuits, that lead to a center point and then out again. There has been a resurgence of interest in the labyrinth in recent years, perhaps spurred by an innate need for a spiritual practice in the midst of an active life. Thus, they are likely to be found not only on church grounds but within civic centers and near hospitals.

Walking the labyrinth forms a metaphor for life as we meet people coming and going. The walk is meant to be slow and purposeful. As a prayer practice, it is a three-part process. At the entrance, we pause to ask God's blessing on our journey. In the center, we pause to pray for openness to what God has to reveal to us. Upon exiting, we pause to ask God to show us what we should take away from the experience and back into our ordinary lives.

SILENCE

Several years ago, I received a request to direct a women's retreat based on Barbara Brown Taylor's book *When God Is Silent*. While meeting with the planning team, I was taken aback by the lengthy discussion about whether or not to include the word "silent" in the title of the retreat. There was a concern that the weekend would be perceived as completely silent, something the group felt would intimidate a number of women. Others pointed out how the word might dredge up painful memories for those who were subjected to silence as a punishment when they were growing up. This was all news to me, as I have savored the experience of silence since I was a small child. A natural introvert, I often sought quiet places in which to withdraw when the sounds of a large family became a bit much.

In the first chapter of her book, Barbara Brown Taylor describes the famine in our world that makes silence such an endangered reality. Part of it, she says, is our addiction to noise. In Chapter 4, I referred to Gordon Hempton's distinction between sound and noise. Quieting the noise in our own heads makes space for silence that might be welcomed or feared. No wonder the practice of silence is such a key to spiritual practice. Nothing will whittle down our defenses and break through to our false selves like the regular immersion into silence. The poet, Rainer Maria Rilke, expresses this beautifully:

I want to unfold.
Let no place in me hold itself closed,
for where I am closed, I am false.
I want to stay clear in your sight.

Like most spiritual practices, the way to start with silence is with small steps. If it does intimidate, we might try it in five-minute segments and gradually increase the time spent with a cessation of noise. Teresa of Ávila was fond of describing the soul as "shy." Little bits of silence might entice it to come forward a bit more, opening itself further and further like a flower unfolding its petals in the warmth of the sun.

SOLITUDE

The late Henri Nouwen noted that solitude is essential to the spiritual life; it is virtually impossible to cultivate one without it. In Chapter 2 we looked at how Jesus walked the tightrope between seclusion and engagement, between his time alone and with others. As noted earlier, his instruction about prayer and the "inner room" was not a reference to a physical space but to the heart. We generally don't find our way toward it while in the middle of center ring. It takes moving away from the nucleus of activity and involvement in order to find space and time on our own.

Like the practice of silence, the pursuit of solitude can be daunting and even repugnant to some. Finding solitary time and space is also harder than ever, thanks to the ever-present reality of cell phones. They are creating an aversion to solitude, something I once heard from a college professor about her students and the use of social media. She described how they not only spend inordinate amounts of time checking Twitter, Facebook, Instagram, and other sites, but will also *pretend* to be doing so when alone so as to not appear as "losers." Talk about putting on a performance to meet the expectation of others!

Nouwen describes the progressive nature of solitude and how we learn to develop an attentiveness toward God's voice with each experience. The first step might feel daunting and even like a waste of time. It might also unleash thoughts and feelings that have remained submerged in the midst of engagement with the people and activities in center ring. Faithfulness to the practice means stepping out again and again until, over time, it becomes as much a necessity as a discipline. Even if we do not feel much immediate satisfaction in our solitude, Nouwen writes, "we realize that a day without [it] is less 'spiritual' than a day with it" (*Making All Things New*).

VISIO DIVINA

Throughout the centuries, artwork has opened up insight and imagination through the depiction of religious themes. *Visio divina* ("divine seeing") is a way of praying with images. Like *lectio divina*, this form of prayer invites us into contemplation by deepening our sight lines and going beyond first glimpses. We move into the image and let go of initial impressions in order to let it evoke new ways of seeing or reflecting upon a biblical account or the life a holy person.

Icons are a revered tradition in the Eastern Orthodox tradition and might be considered doorways to the sacred. My dear friend Father Bill McNichols is a renowned iconographer who describes the power of icons to bring us into the presence of holy people and inviting conversation with them in the midst of ordinary life. Along with other forms of sacred art, they also stir the imagination by presenting visual images of scenes from the Bible and the lives of the saints in ways that resonate with our own lives. McNichols' website (frbillmcnichols-sacredimages.com) offers a display of familiar spiritual themes, such as the Sacred Heart of Jesus, as well as more contemporary ones. The latter includes a beautiful rendering of Saint Toribio Romo y González, protector of immigrants, and a haunting image of Matthew Shepard, the young Wyoming man who was tortured and murdered simply because he was gay.

Art doesn't need to be explicitly religious to be spiritual, however. Photographs of natural landscapes, such as the beautiful ones Ron has taken, awaken an appreciation for the glory of nature. Sculpture generates an appreciation for the wondrous working of the human body. Whatever form it takes, artwork can focus us toward prayer and contemplation in a fresh and creative way.

CONTEMPLATION

I am placing the practice of contemplation last, as it sums up all of the above as well as the entire focus of this book. I think I best understood contemplation as a child. My family home included a large backyard with a gorgeous garden tended with love by my mother. Some of my most memorable moments were spent in that garden; I consider it the site of my first spiritual awakening. One day, while sitting beside the roses, I had a distinct awareness of a divine presence. I didn't question it but simply took in the experience and enjoyed it. While I was way too young to articulate it, I was immersed in a form of contemplation—a wordless way of being in the moment and resting in God's love.

There is a lovely Hasidic saying that goes, "Behind every blade of grass stands an angel telling it to grow." This is an expansive view of nature and its immensely spiritual substance. Is it any wonder that so many of us find our spiritual balance restored while seated on a beach or hiking through the mountains? Jesus' call to "the better part" was one toward rest and the discovery of gentleness and humility. It is a far cry from media messages enticing us toward more stuff to do, want, possess, and protect. Thomas Merton described contemplation as a "loving sense of this life and this presence and this eternity." It is a simple yet profound way of being in the moment, savoring every gift God bestows upon us.

In his book *Music of Silence*, David Steindl-Rast notes the literal meaning of contemplation as a continuous "putting together" in some way. In the contemplative life, "we continuously measure what we are doing in time against the now that doesn't pass away. We strive continuously to tune in to God's creative Spirit, God's will, God's plan, and to let it give shape to reality 'on earth as it is in heaven.'" In short, contemplation weaves together vision and action, center ring and the periphery, Martha and Mary. It is all about the "better part" that comes when we seek, find, and incorporate spiritual balance into our lives.

BIBLIOGRAPHY

Armbrecht, Ann. *Thin Places: A Pilgrimage Home.*
New York: Columbia University Press. 2009.

Bennett-Goleman, Tara. *Emotional Alchemy: How the Mind Can Heal the Heart.* New York: Harmony Books. 2001.

Borg, Marcus. *The Heart of Christianity: Discovering a Life of Faith.*
New York: HarperCollins. 2003.

Bourgeault, Cynthia. *Centering Prayer and Inner Awakening.*
Lanham: Cowley Publishing. 2004.

Breathnach, Sarah Ban. *The Simple Abundance Journal of Gratitude.*
New York: Warner Books, Inc. 1996.

Chodron, Pema. *When Things Fall Apart: Heart Advice for Difficult Times.*
Boston: Shambhala Publications. 1997.

Cox, Harvey. *Common Prayers: Faith, Family, and a Christian's Journey through the Jewish Year.* New York: Houghton Mifflin. 2001.

Flinders, Carol Lee. *Enduring Grace: Living Portraits of Seven Women Mystics.* New York: HarperCollins. 1993.

Godwin, Gail. *Heart: A Natural History of the Heart-filled Life.*
New York: HarperCollins. 2001.

Hendricks, Kathy. *Prayers and Rituals for the Home: Celebrating the Life and Times of Your Family.* New London: Twenty-Third Publications. 2013.

Hendricks, Ron and Kathy. *The Long Road to Oklahoma: Images and Impressions of Our Trip across America.* Denver: KMHendricks, Inc. 2011.

LeClaire, Anne D. *Listening Below the Noise: A Meditation on the Practice of Silence.* New York: HarperCollins. 2009.

Loder, Ted. *Guerrillas of Grace: Prayers for the Battle.* Minneapolis: Augsburg Books. 1981.

Mueller, Wayne. *Learning to Pray: How We Find Heaven on Earth.* New York: Bantam Books. 2003.

Mueller, Wayne. *Sabbath: Finding Rest, Renewal, and Delight in Our Busy Lives.* New York: Bantam Books. 1999.

Nouwen, Henri J.M. *Making All Things New: An Invitation to the Spiritual Life.* New York: HarperCollins. 1981.

Steindl-Rast, David. *Common Sense Spirituality: The Essential Wisdom of David Steindl-Rast.* New York: Crossroad. 2008.

Steindl-Rast, David. *Gratefulness, the Heart of Prayer:
An Approach to Life in Fullness*. Mahwah: Paulist Press. 1984.

Steindl-Rast, David. *Music of Silence: A Sacred Journey through the Hours
of the Day*. Berkeley: Ulysses Press. 1998.

Tasto, Maria. *The Transforming Power of Lectio Divina: How to Pray
with Scripture*. New London: Twenty-Third Publications. 2013.

Thich Nhat Hanh. *The Miracle of Mindfulness: A Manual on Meditation*.
Boston: Beacon Press. 1981.